FRONT PAGE MARRIAGE

FRONT PAGE MARRIAGE

JHAN ROBBINS

G. P. PUTNAM'S SONS
NEW YORK

Library of Congress Cataloging in Publication Data

Robbins, Jhan.
    Front page marriage.

    Bibliography: p.
    1. Hayes, Helen, 1900–   . 2. MacArthur, Charles, 1895–1956—
Biography—Marriage.
3. Actors—United States—Biography. 4. Dramatists, American—
20th century—Biography—Marriage.
I. Title.
PN2287.H35R6   1982   792'.028'0924 [B]   81-17748
ISBN 0-399-12691-0   AACR2

PRINTED IN THE UNITED STATES OF AMERICA
Second Impression

Contents

To Helen Hayes MacArthur
First Lady

Foreword

On August 17, 1928, newspapers throughout the country revealed that actress Helen Hayes and playwright Charles MacArthur had exchanged marriage vows before a retired New York City magistrate. The twenty-seven year-old bride was then winning applause in the long-running melodrama, *Coquette*, and was well on her way to the title First Lady of the Theatre. Charlie, her thirty-one-year-old husband and coauthor of the recently opened smash hit *The Front Page*, was heralded as a unique, daring writer of cynical comedy.

The wedding announcement caused the couple's close friends and associates to make downbeat predictions. The union was appallingly ill suited to both and destined to instant and spectacular failure. "It can't possibly succeed," they all agreed. "Except for being connected with the theatre those two belong in completely different worlds."

Never was a wedding greeted with more gloomy

wisecracks by more brilliant wits. The skeptics started a *Poor Helen-Charlie Club*. Robert Benchley, the bridegroom's former roommate, was designated as unofficial president. The satirical social critic said, "Helen's bouquet was inappropriate. It should have been tied with an old typewriter ribbon and an empty flask shoved down among the pale pink roses. What on earth are they doing together? Charlie's a man of the world, and she makes Pollyanna seem like a painted hussy."

Actress Tallulah Bankhead exclaimed, "Charlie Mac-Arthur is a well-known skirt-chaser. He has roamed around New York town with Bea Lillie, Dorothy Parker, and dozens of other well-ripened females. I surely thought naive little Helen was saving herself for the boy next door."

Other comments were equally sarcastic:

"He is one of the Algonquin Round Table's most unprintable quipsters. Helen leaves the room when anyone mentions 'farmer's daughter.' "

"He swills alcohol by the gallon. She gets intoxicated inhaling malted milk."

"He thrives on stimulating company. That goody-goody virgin's idea of fun is to sit home and wash her hair."

It is hard to say who was the rudest. There was an undeclared competition for that, too. Yet when the marriage was ended by death twenty-eight years later, some of the prophets of doom were still alive to eat their words. The marriage had been a huge if unorthodox success and a happy one. Shortly after MacArthur's funeral in 1956, Tallulah Bankhead, whose uninhibited speech and behavior made her a legend on the Broadway stage, said, "Darling, that merger almost restores my faith. Not only was it made in heaven, but when He made it, God was even wiser than I am. What sheer inspiration joining those two together."

I have written newspaper and magazine articles about Helen Hayes. Two of them were "as told to" and carried her by-line. I thoroughly enjoyed those assignments. I talked to many intimate friends of the MacArthurs, to their relatives, and to dozens of people who worked beside them.

Over the years, I have often written about heads of state, leaders in the arts, politics, and industry. I discovered that it is rare indeed to find a celebrity without numerous detractors. Charles MacArthur had very few, and Helen Hayes—none.

When I told her that I was writing this book, I mentioned that the previous Sunday a small boy had trouble pronouncing my year-old daughter's name properly. Instead of "Kate," he kept calling her "Cake." Helen, who is an avid baseball fan, said, "Cake Robbins! What a wonderful name for a shortstop. By the time she's in her twenties, I bet there'll be lots of women in the major leagues. If she's half good and with a name like that she's got it made. Cake Robbins! "

Asked about the audiences that had watched her entertain them, she replied feelingly, "What I'm proudest of in America is Americans. I know the American people from having trouped around the country for more than fifty years, and there are no better people anywhere. The essence of an American is courage and kindness. I know it doesn't sound right to say that when you look at the headlines in the papers. But those, unfortunately, are the splashy events. There's not much written about the majority of Americans, who are secret doers of good—the secret good, good people. They don't make any noise, and they don't make any fuss, and they are very serious about their country and their politics. I know so many like that, and I consider them the typical Americans."

You can see why I stand in awe of her. Not only is she the first lady of the theatre, but I found that her incongruous marriage to Charles MacArthur was one of the most tender, passionate, and dramatic unions in modern history, well worth this record.

Jhan Robbins

Goldsboro, North Carolina

'Tis a much known passioned fact
That love-blind opposites do attract
And thence breathe many a romantic act. . . .

—Old English Song

1

The Prince of Wit

The unpredictable, mischievous wit of Helen Hayes's husband was apparent early. When Charles MacArthur was eight years old, Georgiana, his mother, who had given birth to seven children of her own, agreed to be a midwife to a neighbor that lived down the road. The unborn infant delayed its appearance. For weeks the conversation at the supper table revolved around the protracted pregnancy. The Reverand William MacArthur, Charlie's father, grumbled that his wife spent too much time at the woman's house. Amiably the neighbor moved in with the MacArthurs so that Georgiana could tend to her endless household chores and still be close to the expectant mother.

One afternoon while the lady was taking a nap, Mrs. MacArthur went shopping. That was when young Charlie decided to act. Stealthily, the boy placed a small pillow next to the sleeping woman, covered it up and ran to fetch his father who was out visiting a backsliding member of his evangelist church.

"It's finally here!" the boy shouted gleefully. William came at once. Charlie whispered that his father could peek but cautioned him not to disturb the slumbering pair. The elder MacArthur tiptoed into the room and saw the tiny lump. He oohed and ahed under his breath and retreated silently. It was only when Georgiana returned a few minutes later that Charlie's prank was discovered. The reverend promptly reached for his leather strap, but at that moment the baby, at long last, decided that his time had arrived.

"Charlie was saved from a licking," said Ben Hecht, his longtime friend and collaborator. "But I really wonder if he would have been whipped very hard. Nobody, but nobody, could be angry with him for very long. Charlie's high-spirited humor was always kind—it never hurt."

Charles MacArthur's exuberant escapades are now part of history. Time has dimmed them. It is a little difficult to understand that he was so hilariously funny or how anyone was gullible enough to fall victim to his pranks. It was a simpler day. People were more easily amused and dignity more tempting to affront. Today, there just may not be sufficient time to allow for it. Yet, the MacArthur legends grow more precious, just as faded antique toys have become priceless heirlooms.

Charlie's mother, Georgiana Welstead MacArthur, one of nineteen children, had been very good-looking in her youth, but poverty, hard work, and childbearing had made much of her former attractiveness disappear. Still, when she had time to comb her hair and don her "going-to-church frock," her former beauty was still apparent.

Her father, who was English, had been a professional soldier and had served in India. Georgiana liked to boast that when he was a sub-lieutenant he had rescued three enlisted men and had been decorated for his bravery.

Another story about her heroic parent that she enjoyed telling concerned a horse he had once been assigned. Welstead had been issued a very cantankerous mare, and his commanding officer, who was named Gotham, constantly ridiculed his riding performance. In exasperation, the sub-lieutenant christened the mount Gotham. When word leaked out, he was asked to explain his actions. He thought fast and said, "No! No! It's not named after Captain Gotham. Heaven forbid. I'd never, never do such a scandalous thing. Its name is God Damn! Perhaps when you say it rapidly it may sound like Gotham?"

Very likely Charlie inherited his keen sense of humor from this grandfather. Another quality that was undoubtedly passed on was extreme stoicism. One day Welstead was thrown by God Damn Gotham, as the horse had come to be called. The result was two broken legs. Not a sound was heard as he bit on a bullet as a fellow officer pushed the bones back into place.

Charlie was equally impassive when a boil the size of a lemon appeared on his back. Although the seven-year-old boy was in severe pain, he was determined to suffer in silence. An alarmed Georgiana was about to take her ailing son to the local doctor, but the youngster's preacher-father insisted that the carbuncle was

God's way of showing that the boy had sinned. Instead of giving the boy proper medical attention, he carried the stricken lad to a bare platform in the shed. Underneath it Reverend MacArthur set out several naptha flares. Then he called members of his congregation to come and pray.

For seven days and nights they begged the Lord to save the young transgressor. Their hosannas and hallelujahs grew louder as they watched the boil get larger and larger until it resembled a grapefruit. Still the feverish and now debilitated Charlie refused to do any moaning. He tried to turn his head, but the carbuncle was too huge to allow for any movement. Instead, he winked weakly at the persevering and perspiring congregation.

At the week's end the boil burst open, which was taken to be a miraculous sign that the sinner had been saved. Reverend MacArthur rapturously joined his flock as they all rejoiced. A relieved Charlie jumped off the platform, bowed to his father's disciples, and waved merrily toward the rotting rafters.

The Reverend William MacArthur's parents had emigrated from Aberdeen, Scotland. After living in Canada they settled on a Pennsylvania farm, where they raised corn, oats, and wheat. At an early age William decided that he, too, would till the soil. It was said that when he was eighteen years old, he and his mule could outfurrow anyone in the county. He seemed to be contented in his work; however, the tall, lean, loquacious young man had serious doubts about what he was doing. One day his threshing machine caught fire. As he watched it burn, he decided that his mission in life was to save souls from entering a flaming hell. On the spot he ordained himself a minister and went forth to rescue sinners.

He headed for Chicago, which he heard was a mecca for the unredeemed. Arriving in the Windy City, he tried to borrow $100 from a storefront bank. The stern-looking manager explained that since MacArthur had no collateral, the loan must be refused. The rejection did not quell William's effusiveness, and standing before the banker's desk, he sermonized for more than an hour. When he discovered that the financier had not been to church for years, he shouted, "Hellfire and damnation!" The startled line of people standing in front of the teller's cage watched the bank manager fall to his knees as he and MacArthur prayed out loud. Then the preacher helped the man to his feet as the manager began to write out a loan.

"True, I didn't get all the money I asked for," Charlie's father later reported. "But he did loan me $25 and that was better than nothing. What's more important, I had the wonderful satisfaction of bringing a straggler back to the fold."

After the itinerant preacher felt he had saved enough of the sinful in Chicago, he backtracked east, always imploring disbelievers to repent their evil ways and seek the Lord. He at last settled in what was then the busy little riverport of Nyack, New York, where he decided that his special fundamentalist skills were needed.

Charlie was born en route in Scranton, Pennsylvania, on November 5, 1895, the fifth of seven children—Alfred, Marguerite, Telfer, Helen, Charles, John, Roderick. He recalled that his God-fearing father often brought sinners into their ramshackle manse and ordered his wife to feed them. His theory was that it was easier to redeem them after she filled their bellies.

"My mother was an ingenious woman," said Charlie. "She had to be. We were very poor, but she always found ways to put food on the table. Some days the larder was so empty that she had to tie a piece of cabbage onto a string and tip it into a boiling pot of water. She would then serve us 'soup à la cabbage.' I remember that on many nights, I couldn't fall asleep because my hungry stomach made so much noise."

The reverend wanted Charlie to become a minister. He sent him to Wilson Memorial Academy in Nyack, a school for missionaries. The curriculum was devoted to Bible study. Young MacArthur found time to excel in jest and high jinks. The other students referred to him as Chick, the Holy Joker. Tad Smith, a classmate, recalled, "Chick was the life of the school. We sure needed him, as the place seemed more like a funeral parlor. Everything he did and said was a barrel of fun.

"There was one thing he couldn't stand and that was a show-off. Ichabod, a kid in class, used to constantly brag about his father's automobile. Remember, in those days owning a car was a pretty rare thing. Itchy would rave on and on: how much it cost, how fast it went, how many people it could carry. Well, Chick finally had it up to his ears. That night he got a few of the fellows together. We all got candles and stole up to Itchy's house, which was close by. His father kept the car in the barn—I think it was a Model A Ford. Then, with Chick directing the operation, we quietly took it apart piece by piece. We carried the parts up to the loft, where we reassembled it. As if that wasn't enough for

Chick, he left on the seat a piece of cardboard on which he had printed: 'Proverbs 17:21.'*

"For weeks afterward it was the main topic of conversation—'How did the auto get up the ladder?' Chick was suspected of being the mastermind, but nobody could prove it. Besides, Wilson Academy took a dim view of the horseless carriage. They felt it was 'Satan's chariot.' "

Charlie may not have been punished for that deed, but he was not so lucky when a few weeks later he struck again. Another of the school's declared enemies was alcohol. Lectures were delivered daily on the evils of liquor. Right after one of these tirades young MacArthur was called on to give a recitation from his favorite book. From the *Rubaiyat of Omar Khayam* he selected an extended passage beginning with Stanza VII, "Come, fill the cup. . . ."

This time a very indignant teacher applied the switch to the fourteen-year-old boy. Charlie said later that despite a sore backside, the licking was well worth the look on the man's face.

Clarence Heimer, one of the instructors, decided to conduct a schoolwide literary contest and ordered each student to write a short story. The boy who turned in the best one would be made editor of the new school newspaper. Charlie won. His story about a man who found salvation on a windswept desert island sounded so professional that his father accused him of copying it out of a magazine. Charlie denied it. After Charlie edited his first issue of the newspaper, William MacAr-

---

*"A stupid son is a grief to a father; and the father of a fool has no joy."

thur realized the youngster had told the truth and half-apologized. The next time the boy did something wrong the father gave him half as many lashes.

"My reaction," said Charlie, "was to half-smile and half-cry."

One of the few recorded occasions on which Charlie was almost serious occurred when he was instructed to write an editorial on God for the school newspaper. "He didn't treat the matter lightly," said Tad Smith. "Usually, he would dash off his assignments in a matter of minutes. This time he just thought and thought. He finally handed it in. He had compared God to Santa Claus. Like Santa, he wrote, God really loved everybody and had gifts for every man, woman, and child. It's not that Charlie was being disrespectful. Not at all. He told me he sure got it from his father when he went home."

The proposed editorial was not published, but many years later, when MacArthur was collaborating with Ben Hecht on *Ladies and Gentlemen*, he wanted to use some of his God–Santa Claus lines in the play. Hecht agreed that there was a valid resemblance but cautioned against using it because he felt that the audience would regard it as being too agnostic.

"Instead," recalled Hecht, "we said something about Mrs. Roosevelt coming to town. In his own way Charlie was a deeply religious man. We discussed the subject often. He didn't believe in gibberish jargon or making a man feel guilty that he was an everlasting sinner. None of that for our Charlie. He really believed that God was a merry old man who loved everybody."

Attendance at Wilson Academy made MacArthur realize that he did not want to seek a religious career.

"Words have long appealed to me," he once told Alexander Woollcott. "At an early age I made up my mind to be a writer. I guess it all started when my mother read some poetry of Henry Wadsworth Longfellow to me. I can still remember her sweet, sad voice reciting ["My Lost Youth"]: 'A boy's will is the wind's will / And the thoughts of youth are long, long thoughts.' "

Charlie's older brothers also shunned the ministry. They left home in their late teens. Alfred went to work for the Central Life Insurance Company of Chicago. Telfer founded a weekly newspaper in eastern Illinois. When Charlie was seventeen, he, too, left Nyack and worked one summer for Telfer. Then he became a $10 a week reporter for the *City Press*, a Chicago daily. Edgar Leighton, who shared a desk with him, said, "In those days there were easy ways of putting a story together. You'd mostly sit on your duff and write a routine couple of lines. But that wasn't this guy's method. No siree. He'd actually get firsthand details and write a ripsnorting yarn. He had a keen ear for the way people spoke, and he wrote it down letter-perfect. You could tell then that he was climbing the ladder to the very top."

Charlie took time out to join the Illinois militia and was dispatched to Mexico to help capture Pancho Villa. "He was probably the best-known private over there," said Lorenzo Del Vecchio, who served with him. "We were both in the cavalry, but MacArthur didn't get to spend much time on a horse. He was a steady visitor to the stockade. He did such wild things like painting epaulets and gold bars on his guardhouse fatigues. He'd then pretend that he was a captain. You'd think that it would be easy to spot the imposter. Somehow he made it work. I tell you that guy was a genius.

"Once he got more than a hundred signatures—officers included—on a petition that would guarantee hot water bottles and belly dancers for every tent. He would lead the other prisoners and military police in hymn singing. The MPs grew so fond of him that it was not uncommon to see Charlie and a band of them sit in the orderly room nursing bottles of rye and quietly singing 'Nearer, My God, to Thee.' "

The *Chicago Tribune* of November 2, 1916 carried an intriguing story about the errant soldier: "Charles MacArthur, associate editor of *The Cavalryman*, the publication of the 1st Cavalry, for whom a provost guard had been searching for several days, returned to camp yesterday with a thrilling tale of having been stabbed in the arm with a morphine needle by a vampire woman and set adrift in an open boat."

Years later, just after his marriage to Helen Hayes, Charlie and his recent bride were celebrating New Year's Eve in Chicago's Tavern Club. About five minutes before midnight Charlie spotted Colonel Milton Foreman, the officer in charge of his cavalry outfit. He said to his wife, "Come and meet my first colonel." He then introduced her to Foreman and added, "I fought with you in Mexico."

The colonel beamed happily and replied, "Any man who was in my outfit is most welcome. Do sit down. By the way what's your name?"

"Private Charles MacArthur at your service," said Charlie, snapping to attention.

Foreman blanched, looked at MacArthur with alarm, then without saying another word ran from the table as fast as he could. He reached the exit as the band was playing "Auld Lang Syne." He turned, stared at Charlie again, shook his head furiously, and quickly left the room.

A very surprised MacArthur asked Helen, "Do you suppose he's still angry about that harmless little homecoming incident?"

When Foreman had returned to the United States following the Mexican campaign, he was given a tickertape parade down Chicago's Michigan Avenue. Charlie, who was about to be discharged from the army, decided to lead the procession—he said he wanted to demonstrate his patriotism. He borrowed a dilapidated Ford and decorated it with a huge American flag. Then he chained two ladies who worked at Madam Farrington's brothel to the car, to represent Mexican prisoners. And to the thousands of spectators who lined the streets he shouted, "Long live tinpants Milton Foreman!"

When America entered World War I, Charlie signed up immediately. This time he served with the Rainbow Division and saw action in the Meuse-Argonne and Château-Thierry. Lieutenant William Cavanaugh, who was once in charge of his unit, said, "All kidding aside, MacArthur was a born soldier, He could have gone far in the army, but he didn't take himself with a straight face, or for that matter, anyone else. He had a lot of raw courage—was always one of the first men in our outfit to somehow land in enemy territory. I remember one time he met a German corporal, and they tried to find out whose field equipment was tougher. They took off their helmets, placed them on the ground and started shooting at them, making bets about which helmet was pierced with the most holes."

Just after the fighting ceased, the men in Charlie's

battery urged him to write a book about their army experiences. They chipped in to have it privately printed. It was originally called *A Bug's Eye View of the War* and then it was changed to *War Bugs*. A Chicago newspaper reviewer who was given a copy said, "It's the most hilarious account I've read about our soldiers. Not that the author pulls any punches about dying in the trenches. But he even manages to find laughter when the shells are flying . . . a warm salute to Private MacArthur."

Back in the Midwest Charlie became a reporter for the *Chicago Herald-Examiner*. Later he joined the editorial staff of the *Chicago Tribune*. The young journalist quickly developed a cynical attitude and an irreverent approach to almost everything. He was neither awed by wealth nor impressed by position and thought nothing of poking fun in his copy at influential legislators and financiers.

His news stories were widely acclaimed. Soon he was one of the highest-paid reporters in Chicago. He received $100 a week from the *Tribune*, an unheard-of salary. When old-hand newspapermen get together, they invariably reminisce about Charles MacArthur. "Most of the time," said Mike Rotunno, a veteran Chicago newspaper photographer, "stories get inflated over the years. In Charlie's case it's the other way around. With him it's impossible to overstate!"

One of MacArthur's first assignments upon joining the *Herald-Examiner* was to interview an Arab prince whose claim to fame was that he had recently inherited $20 million from his grandfather. The young reporter raced to the elegant hotel where the wealthy potentate was staying and was ushered up to a plush suite. After half an hour of sterile conversation Charlie realized that he did not have much of a story. What to do?

The prince excused himself to go to the bathroom. Charlie said he fooled around with the observation that perhaps he could write that even people of royal blood have to relieve themselves. However, upon closer reflection, he decided that his city editor would not buy that. When a chambermaid came in to clean the rooms, he hit upon a brilliant idea: what if the Arab nobleman, who was heir to a throne, married the poor American maid? He would surely get a front-page by-line. He screened her quickly and in minutes learned her life's history.

When the prince returned, MacArthur started to list her virtues. True, she was very plump, but a recent University of Chicago survey revealed that fat girls made the best wives; she was an orphan, so he would have no in-law annoyances; she was very quiet and would not present a disciplinary problem; she rarely got sick and had a good set of teeth. "All in all," said Charlie assuredly, "she's a great catch. Will you marry her?"

The prince, whose command of English was very limited, nodded. MacArthur interpreted the gesture as assent. He was delighted and could already savor the raise he would receive when he brought in his story. Unfortunately, the prince's chief aide, who was present, understood English. He quickly vetoed Charlie's weird proposition.

Another MacArthur anecdote that is told and retold concerns a dentist who had been accused of raping a patient. Ben Hecht, who worked for a rival Chicago newspaper, recalled that after Charlie had interviewed the victim and the alleged culprit, he turned in three hundred words of copy about the unsavory incident. "Charlie's lead," said Hecht, "was memorable: 'Tooth doctor fills wrong cavity.'"

The *Tribune* assigned MacArthur to cover the hanging of a youth named Frank Piano, who had been found guilty of stabbing a friend to death. Charlie did not want to write the standard execution story, and so, one day while playing gin rummy with the doomed man, he concocted a bizzare plot. He would arrange for the hangman's rope to be placed near the windpipe instead of the side; he had been told that position would not break the neck and that the victim could be resuscitated.

He convinced the warden that it was all legal and that if he cooperated, he would receive national publicity and his name would instantly become a household word. The covetous warden agreed. Then MacArthur cautioned Piano not to struggle against the rope. "If you're still conscious," he said, "pretend you're dead."

Charlie's next visit was to the condemned man's parents, where he guzzled their Chianti and confided his secret. Right after the make-believe death, Frankie would be cut down, his mother would claim the body, rush it to a waiting van that MacArthur had arranged for, and a doctor with a syringe filled with adrenalin would bring the young man back to life. The Pianos were so exhilarated by the scheme that they planned a gala banquet for the night of the execution. Hundreds of relatives were invited to honor their son's savior. Charlie was to be the guest of honor.

It all sounded so simple. However, MacArthur had

missed one detail: he had failed to take the local sheriff into his confidence. The lawman had learned about the plot and was jealous of the limelight that would surely fall upon the warden. He requisitioned the body while it was still swinging and rushed it to the Cook County Hospital, where it was promptly dissected.

A popular male rendezvous that was frequented by some of the best people in Chicago was Madam Farrington's brothel at Twelfth Street and Michigan Boulevard. A westside alderman who had become prosperous from pork-barreling invited Charlie to be his guest at the posh bordello. The man was a frequent customer and was given preferential treatment. Magnanimously he told MacArthur that he would foot the bill for anything the young reporter selected. He meant any girl. Charlie, who had earned the reputation of being a "skirt-chaser" and "gay-dog," decided to fluster the politician.

"Anything?" he asked.

"Yes, yes," the man replied generously.

Charlie took great care in scrutinizing all the assembled girls. He did this several times. Finally, he said, "I've made up my mind." Then he paused for emphasis. "I'll take . . . the walnut player piano. Please have it delivered to my house."

"For some strange reason MacArthur felt it was the worst crime to pay for trolley rides with real coins," said Victor Boesen, a former Chicago newspaperman. "He showed us how to beat the system. He'd go into the hardware store and buy a pound of slugs. Soon we were all doing it. However, it often cost us more than we would have paid in the first place. He'd insist that we buy the conductor a beer."

While still working on the *Herald-Examiner*, Charlie married Carol Frink, a colleague he had courted at the newspaper's water cooler. Carol, a petite blonde with a fashionable pageboy, usually covered flower shows and cooking demonstrations. MacArthur told her that she was ready for bigger things. He suggested that she dress up as a policeman and make arrests. He was sure that she could write a fabulous story about her breath-taking law-enforcement adventures. Unfortunately, no one took her seriously—the uniform he had rented for her was that of a Texas ranger. Later he urged Carol to pretend to play the French horn with the Chicago Symphony, but the conductor spotted her and chased her out of the concert hall.

The couple were married in New York by Charlie's father. When they returned from a honeymoon to Coney Island, the new bride finally earned a by-line on her paper. " 'By Mrs. Charles MacArthur' . . . I liked him because he smiled wide and often as if he meant it and said nice silly things to make me laugh on days when I felt weepy and blue. . . . He has a special kind of brilliance and is tall, dark and handsome. The way he twists his curly forelock is enough to drive any girl wild."

Charlie felt that his new wife had loads of talent and was destined to write the great American novel. He made her resign her job because he did not think the fast pace of Chicago was the proper place for Carol's "creative genius." He bought her a new typewriter and raccoon coat. Then he shipped her off to a remote part of Michigan, where she could converse with birds and compose without interruption. To make it all possible, he took on an additional job on a weekly newspaper. The strain began to show, and Bugsy Fallon, a prominent safecracker whom Charlie had befriended, said, "Why knock your brains out? I'll take you in as a partner. In my line of work, you have lots of days off and it pays real good."

MacArthur thanked him but replied that he would stick to the newspaper racket. "I know the routine," he told Bugsy. "Besides my fingerprints don't photograph very well."

After several months and much pleading by Charlie, Carol grudgingly sent him the uncompleted first chapter of her manuscript. He showed it to Ben Hecht. "It was lousy," Charlie's friend said. "I tried to let him down easy and told him her stuff was interesting but that the reading public wasn't ready for her special artistic style. I never knew if Charlie realized I was lying. It was as if he didn't want to find out she was a secondrater. He decided to try new stamping grounds, but she was reluctant to go along."

With his wife in Michigan, Charlie said good-bye to his Runyonesque group of companions and headed for New York. There he and Gene Fowler, the eccentric author who had preceded him to the city, resumed their friendship. Fowler said, "With him in it, New York was never again the same: it suddenly improved and became almost bearable."

One of the first things the unrestrained pair did in the Empire City was to get roaring drunk. "Charlie always was an awe-inspiring drinker," said Fowler. "But this time he really tied one on. So did I. Every time my glass of grog would go down as much as a sixteenth of an inch, he'd start pouring. He did the same with his glass, only more frequently. I'd say he was the most creative boozer I've ever met, and I've met most of them. Each time we took a sip, he'd offer a toast. They were all original, never the same.

"I don't fully remember that night, but, I do recall that at one point Charlie insisted that we purchase birthday cakes for all the lonely canines at the ASPCA. At a fancy French bakery we selected about a dozen of the largest and gooiest creations available."

Then a taxi delivered the two men and the pastry to the ASPCA on Fourth Avenue, where Charlie knocked on the door and said to the bewildered porter who opened it, "My good man, we've come to jubilate with your charges."

When MacArthur introduced Fowler, who was called the Baron of Bohemianism, to one of his female friends, she gasped, "No, it can't be possible—another Charles MacArthur!"

And Fowler said, "No, it isn't! When God invented Charlie, not only did He toss away the pattern, but He offered him His job. . . . Like the Creator, never once did I hear Charlie take any credit for his remarkable capers. He was exceedingly self-abasing. He'd say humbly, 'I just stood back looking real Christlike and all the others ganged up and tossed wet horseshit at me.' "

MacArthur began selling short stories to a magazine called *Smart Set* at $60 apiece. H. L. Mencken, who was then the editor, labeled Charlie "an unconstrained virtuoso."

The "unconstrained virtuoso" got an editorial job on the *American Weekly*, a Sunday supplement, syndicated with the Hearst newspapers. The job paid $150 a week. Charlie declared that he would send the bulk of his earnings to Carol. He wrote to her that he had completely reformed and that they would "soon be rolling in riches."

His reformation lasted exactly two paychecks. In a Third Avenue speakeasy he had met a kindred soul who had just perfected a rejuvenating cream extracted from the sex organs of a rare South American snake that he claimed made octogenerians jump about and look like fresh-faced first-time voters. The wonder cream was called Miriko. Charlie decided to join forces with the inventor. He had visions of quick millions that would result from his writing a two-page spread about the product for his magazine.

MacArthur and his new friend arranged a demonstration for *American Weekly* editor Morrill Goddard. Two lovely-looking chorus girls, friends of Charlie, were selected to help demonstrate the miracle cure. They assured the editor that they were really in their eighties but that using Miriko faithfully had radically changed their appearances. "For us it's been like discovering the Fountain of Youth," they recited. Just then a middle-aged woman entered the room. "So there you are!" she shouted. "Behind closed doors with two men!"

Goddard wanted to know why she was seeking those nice old ladies. "Old ladies?" shrieked the woman. "Why they're my twin twenty-one-year-old daughters!"

Charlie wrote Carol about this latest escapade. She threw in the towel. "You'll never grow up," she answered bitterly. "Better we should split." MacArthur, who had grown tired of matrimony even at long distance, agreed. The couple soon drifted apart, but it took many years for Carol to refrain from being called Mrs. Charles MacArthur.

Charlie decided to give up his job and try to become a "flourishing fat-cat freelancer" like Robert Benchley, whom he had met at a cocktail party. The humorist had assured him, "There's a whole country full of gullible suckers who haven't even heard one of your crazy stories. You'll make a mint."

Benchley was so impressed with MacArthur that he offered to share his appartment with Charlie. MacArthur accepted but added a note of caution. "I'm a late sleeper," he warned. "Be careful to boil your eggs very softly and not to scrape the toast!"

Soon the quixotic duo were the talk of the town. No social gathering was considered complete without MacArthur and Benchley. The guests roared at their sallies. The more they spurned invitations, the more intensely they were sought. Benchley once bet his crony $5 that he could say "Shave and a haircut" most of the evening and females would swoon with delight. At a swanky coming-out party MacArthur, by Benchley's count, repeated "Shave and a haircut" fifty-seven times. When the debut was over, a demure young thing said to Benchley, "I could listen to Mr. MacArthur forever. He says such bright things. He was especially wonderful tonight." The loser paid up.

At one time during the three years that Charlie lodged with Benchley he did free-lance work for a public-relations firm that represented among its clients a large cemetery in northern New Jersey. MacArthur was assigned to the account. He had grandiose plans that he carefully discussed with his roommate. Benchley agreed they were stupendous.

Charlie convinced the client that they should establish a poet's corner like the world-famed one in Westminster Abbey and change the name of the burial spot to something more dignified. He suggested Fairview Abbey. Quite pleased, the client agreed. Then MacArthur proposed, "To make Fairview Abbey world-renowned we need a distinguished resident."

His first choice was Henry Wadsworth Longfellow. Charlie had been told that the late poet was buried in Boston, so he dispatched a special-delivery letter to James Curley, the mayor. A " 'grave' error had been committed," he wrote. "Longfellow should have rightly been buried in New Jersey because that had been the poet's sincerest wish. "The mistake should be rectified instantaneously!" he said.

Curley replied that Longfellow was buried in Cambridge, Massachusetts, which was not in his jurisdiction, but that he would discuss the matter with that city's mayor. A week went by without any action. Then MacArthur, assisted by Benchley, sent a series of telegrams to Curley: "If you value your job you will forward the remains immediately!" "Come clean with that body!" "Roll dem bones!" Longfellow remained in Massachusetts. MacArthur sought another job.

Benchley sat regularly for lunch at the exclusive Round Table in the Red Room of Manhattan's Hotel Algonquin. He told his fellow diners about MacArthur. Alexander Woollcott, the leading verbal jouster, instructed him to bring Charlie along. "Anyone who is that good a jokesmith should join us," he said. "Let's look him over."

The Algonquin Round Table, as the clique was called, was once wistfully alluded to by John F. Kennedy. "When I was growing up I had three wishes," he sighed. "I wanted to be a Lindbergh-type hero, learn to speak Chinese, and become a member of the Algonquin Round Table. My father told me that these wiseacres engaged in the world's sharpest repartee. How I admired them."

The regulars in this unique body of wits were Woollcott, Benchley, Ring Lardner, George S. Kaufman, Dorothy Parker, Robert Sherwood, Franklin Pierce Adams, and Edna Ferber. Sometimes guests consisted of Harpo Marx, Paul Robeson, Nunnally Johnson, Noel Coward, Marc Connelly, and Alfred Lunt.

MacArthur bowed low when he was introduced to the group. "I was warned to watch out for your fangs," he said solemnly. "But now I realize that was only a myth. No fangs are visible. Only sabers."

After Charlie passed muster, Woollcott, who became his leading booster, said, "Getting him was the most sagacious brainstorm I ever had. Everyone who knows him lights up when he hears his name and starts talking about him as if he were a marvelous circus that once passed his way. On that very first day, I realized that Charlie was a confusing mixture of Satanic mischief and childlike comic blundering. It was as if he had escaped from Robin Hood's merry band and was vaguely headed for the Holy Land on a pair of rubber-bladed iceskates."

Woollcott was a matchmaker. He decided that Dorothy Parker and Charlie would make a perfect couple. At every opportunity, he pushed them together. Dorothy, who was then selling her short stories, poetry, and essays to leading magazines, was pleased. So was Charlie. In addition to being a versatile writer, she had a lovely face and shapely figure. He also admired her hard-boiled wit and the fact that she was frankly sexual and not afraid to say so, which at that time was unheard-of daring.

At one of the luncheons, she was asked if she had enjoyed a cocktail party she had recently attended. "Enjoyed it!" she replied. "One more drink and I'd have have been under the host!"

At a Halloween party she joined a group of revelers who were "ducking for apples." "Change one letter in that phrase," she said, "and you have the story of my life."

Her wit was so devastating that she often was credited with lines she may not have said: "If all the girls who attended the Yale prom were laid end to end, I wouldn't be a bit surprised." When Charlie was told about the latest Parker barb, he said, "That sounds like Dotty on an off day."

In addition to her forthrightness, he was proud of her strong social concerns and would often say happily that she had been arrested for "sauntering" in a demonstration protesting the execution of the anarchists Nicola Sacco and Bartolomeo Vanzetti. Women pickets were rare and daring then.

Donald Ogden Stewart, the novelist and screenwriter, occasionally joined the group at the Round Table. "Dotty adored Charlie," he said. "And why shouldn't she? He was the best-looking and most gifted male in the group. With her it was a serious, desperate thing. Some of their friends were sure they would soon get married. I knew better. Charlie wasn't ready for another permanent woman. He liked being an extremely eligible bachelor. Besides, legally, he still was wed to that lady in Chicago."

The affair ended when Bea Lillie, the sophisticated British comedienne, entered the picture. She also felt Charlie was "the most marvelous, merriest, masculine answer to my lifetime of prayer."

Here, too, Stewart was skeptical about a serious affiliation. "There was talk that Bea would hook Charlie," he said. "Again I had strong doubts. He was waiting. I had the feeling that when he chose another woman it would not be one of the bright, unpredictable, and unconventional females but a simpler, quiet, and trusting person. What he wanted more than anything else was to make the transition from newsprint bum to being one of the country's leading playwrights. He wanted a woman who felt he could."

MacArthur's brother Alfred was married to the sister of playwright Ned Sheldon. When Alfred introduced MacArthur to Sheldon, he urged the established dramatist, who had been credited with helping to shape the American theatre in the first quarter of the twentieth century, to take Charlie on as a protégé. "I don't think you'll regret it."

Sheldon promised that he would. Although a very severe case of degenerative arthritis developed when Sheldon was still in his thirties and, at the top of his career, forced him to spend his days in bed, his penthouse apartment served as a clearing house for many of the country's leading artists. In addition to total paralysis, he suffered blindness. The only sign of life was his very resonant voice.

He would lie motionless on his high canopied bed and discuss playwriting with the eager MacArthur. He once told producer David Belasco, "Charlie milks me dry with all his passionate questions about our craft. Oh, how he wants to learn. The trouble with him is that he doesn't realize how good he really is. I pray that someday he will discover it."

Ned Sheldon, who had written a dozen successful plays, was credited with helping MacArthur achieve his first Broadway success. Together they collaborated on *Lulu Belle*, which had a moderate run. It opened on February 9, 1926, with a cast of a hundred black and fifteen white actors. The racial attitudes that appeared in the script would be considered outrageous today. Charlie once told Paul Robeson, the black actor and singer, "I apologize for some of the things we said in *Lulu Belle*—'tarbaby,' 'musta'd colored snake charmer,' and 'real nigger style.' Unfortunately, that's the way people talked."

"The only time Charlie acted with restraint was in Sheldon's presence," said Ben Hecht. "I had never seen him toned down by anyone before. The smile went from his face. There was no abstracted pull at his forelock. Charlie looked steadily and humbly at the gentle man, as if he were royalty."

Trying to remember Charlie, whom he loved to exasperation, admiration, and beyond, Hecht sometimes wept. He said that MacArthur enjoyed the fun people and always gave them a good run for laughs. But once in a while, as in his encounter with Sheldon, he found real talent, structure, and steadfastness. He yielded to those qualities. Then he met a woman with all of that and more.

It was Marc Connelly who reported the first encounter between Charles MacArthur and Helen Hayes. "He met her at a party at Neysa's studio," he said. "It was love at first sight, only Charlie, being Charlie, didn't recognize the symptoms right off. It took him awhile to realize how smitten he was. He told me he felt dizzy. He thought it was something he'd eaten."

Neysa McMein, a leading magazine illustrator, held open house every weekday afternoon from four until seven. The most talented people in New York flocked to her studio apartment. Helen, who was then appearing in *To the Ladies*, was taken there by the play's coauthor, Marc Connelly. Some of the others in attendance were Irving Berlin, George Gershwin, Alice Duer Miller, Alexander Woollcott, Robert Benchley, and George S. Kaufman.

Awed by such distinguished company Helen sat quietly in a corner sipping ginger ale and listening to the flow of brilliant conversation. Suddenly, a handsome young man with very curly hair came up to her, held out a dish, and said, "Want a peanut?"

The handsome young man with very curly hair was Charles MacArthur. With great deference she accepted the offering. He then poured several more salted peanuts into her hands and added, looking deep into her eyes, "I wish they were emeralds."

Connelly, who was standing nearby, said, "I was so impressed by that phrase that I wanted to jot it down immediately. The world of lovers is forever in Charlie's debt."

2
The Princess of Broadway

A lthough Helen Hayes has been toasted by presidents and chased by sheikhs," said Al ("Pop") Stern, veteran observer of show-business behavior and possessor of a sixty-eight-year-long career as a stage-doorman, "at age eighty she still has all the kidlike innocence I first saw when she acted in *Pollyanna*. Believe me, on Broadway it's next to impossible to maintain innocence for a week let alone a lifetime. But this is a special kind of lady."

Charles MacArthur, who married the "special kind of lady," solemnly noted that on the day she was born, he was served pot roast, potatoes, and sweet corn—almost unheard-of delicacies in the MacArthur family. "I sure remember that feast," he once told Leland Hayward, his literary agent. "My mother may not have known the reason for it, but I do now. Right from the beginning Helen's been my good-luck charm. When I get back to Nyack, I'm going to thank her for that pot roast."

Helen was born on October 20, 1900, in Washington, D. C. Less than a month later President William McKinley defeated William Jennings Bryan in that year's national election and continued to reside in the nation's capital. Helen's father, Francis V. Brown, did not get to cast a vote, but a pragmatic political canvasser had classified him "Eager to please."

"My father's middle-class ancestors came to America when it was still a crown colony," said Helen. "He married my scamp Irish mother against his parents' wishes. . . . He married for love and to get a home. She married to escape from one."

Brown was chief salesman for a wholesale meat-packing company that specialized in pork products. He was frequently away from home, supervising his staff on the road. Helen remembers that when he was around, he was "fat and jolly . . . a wonderful companion."

Catherine Hayes Brown, her lighthearted, restless, dizzy-minded mother, was an aspiring actress. Her small claim to theatrical fame was that in her youth she had been one of the leads in a local stock-company production of *Damon and Pythias*. She loved to brag that her great-great-aunt, also named Catherine Hayes, had been a singer known professionally as the Erin Swan. "She was the toast of Ireland and England," she would boast. "In America, Catherine was a favorite of the forty-niners. When she toured California, they kept cheering and yelling for her. It wasn't unusual for her to take several dozen curtain calls a night."

Helen's mother was determined to follow the path of her great-great-aunt and become a star. A few years after the birth of her only child, she departed from her dull marriage and rejoined the stock company. At the time, Helen was very unsettled by her absence. Now, she says she understands why she was boarded out: her mother was chasing a rainbow. Dissatisfied with her pedestrian life, she was having her last fling.

Catherine Brown left her young daughter in her mother's charge. Fortunately, Graddy Hayes was an ideal caretaker. Helen remembers her as being "warm and safe and loving . . . the last generation of real grandmothers."

Mrs. Brown's hopes for theatrical advancement were quickly dashed as she was assigned subordinate roles. Stripped of her illusions, she returned home a very dejected woman. Her spirits rose when she thought she recognized that her daughter was a born actress. She laid out a disciplined program of instruction. Francis Brown would return from a sales trip and find his wife almost too busy to say hello. She was coaching the child on how to project her voice, how to bow artistically, how to recite poetry eloquently. The youngster dutifully imitated the older woman but, after a short time, clearly surpassed her. Mrs. Brown was now determined that what she considered the child's natural acting ability should be recognized as soon as possible.

When Helen was five years old, her mother learned that a local theatrical group needed a small child to take the part of Prince Charles in a production they were giving of *The Royal Family*. She thought her daughter would be ideal for the role. Helen was selected. Her appearance, however, did not give her the exposure Mrs. Brown had hoped for. Like other stage-struck mothers, she devised a plan, convinced that all the child needed was "one good break." She enrolled Helen in Miss Minnie Hawkes's School of Dance because she knew that the school conducted an annual May charity pageant that received wide publicity.

The first time Helen appeared in it, she pranced on the stage and did an Irish jig, wearing a green dress with spangled shamrocks. She whirled about so rapidly that she was on the stage for less than a minute and went completely unnoticed. A newspaper story that described the event failed to mention her. Mrs. Brown was undaunted and started thinking about the next May ball. She decided that her daughter was not destined to be a dancer. Instead, she encouraged her to try singing. She convinced Miss Minnie Hawkes that the child warbled as "sweetly as a love-starved lark."

For months Mrs. Brown instructed Helen in how to impersonate Annabelle Whitford, then the leading lady of the Ziegfeld Follies. She taught her daughter the celebrated star's walk, fluffed her hair up high, and painstakingly rehearsed her bathing-beauty number. Helen sang:

> *Why do they call me the Gibson Girl,*
> *The Gibson Girl, the Gibson Girl?*
> *What is the matter with Mr. Ibsen?*
> *Why Dana Gibson?*
> *Just wear a blank expression*
> *And a monumental curl,*
> *Walk with a bend in your back and*
> *They'll call you a Gibson Girl.*

The following May, Mrs. Brown made sure that her daughter would be recognized. Helen, decked out in a low-cut black taffeta bathing suit, was on center stage for more than five minutes. She slinked about, paused invitingly, and cast seductive glances while mimicking the famous Follies star. When she finished her routine, the audience was so enchanted that it refused to allow her to leave the stage. Helen took eight bows. Lew Fields of the vaudeville comedy team Weber and Fields was playing in Washington that week and had been invited to attend the recital. He was properly impressed.

After the performance Fields sent Miss Hawkes a note saying that if the Browns were interested in a stage career for their daughter, they should come and see him in New York. Mrs. Brown was indeed interested, but Helen's father protested that the child was too young and New York a long way off.

Surprisingly, Mrs. Brown did not offer much resistance. Helen's success that afternoon convinced her that soon there would be other offers. She felt the child needed more polish. For the next six months she and her daughter continued to visit the dancing school. Roly-poly Minnie Hawkes said, "I don't feel I should take all the credit for giving the child her chance. To tell the truth, I felt there were other girls among my pupils who appeared more likely to be headed for stardom. But I will say that I predicted tremendous success for Helen's mother. Mrs. Brown, bless her heart, was the greatest firebrand I've ever seen. She knew just how to push her daughter into the limelight. Personally, she was a dear, charming woman, but where Helen was concerned, she let nothing and nobody stand in her way!"

When the time came for Helen to start first grade, her mother, who ordinarily frowned on organized religion, selected Holy Cross, a Roman Catholic academy. At the time, there was great unrest about smallpox vaccinations being required for all students attending district public schools. Washington was full of rumors about dirty needles mutilating children's arms. She was having none of that for her daughter! Moreover, Holy Cross had a fine dramatic program. While there, Helen appeared as Peaseblossom in *A Midsummer Night's Dream*.

It was also at Holy Cross that Helen was exposed to the Roman Catholic faith. "It's been with me ever since," she said. "It has supported me through tragedy and misfortune. I was so impressed with the dedication of the nuns that I dreamed of becoming one of them. I wore out the knees of my stockings with my constant praying."

Mrs. Brown's plans did not include her daughter answering God's call. She was listening on another line. She had just been told by the producer of a local acting group that he wanted Helen for the lead in a play he was casting for summer stock. As bait he offered Mrs. Brown a minor speaking part. She was delighted and assured her doubtful husband that not only would the child be near home but that she, the mother, would be close by to supervise her. He realized it was pointless to argue and reluctantly gave his permission.

For the next few summers, Helen played leading roles in *Mrs. Wiggs of the Cabbage Patch, The Prince and the Pauper*, and *Little Lord Fauntleroy*. Her father still had objections about his daughter becoming an actress, but whenever he was in town, he would proudly watch her perform. His Elks chapter was conducting a gala festival, and he wanted Helen to participate. Mrs. Brown put her foot down. "No!" she said firmly. "It's much too amateurish! She is a professional!"

Helen acted the part of Lord Fauntleroy so convincingly that when the grandfather spoke to her harshly in the first act, a young boy sitting in the audience shouted, "Why does he have to be so mean to somebody as nice as you?"

Already a masterful trouper, Helen usually ignored such interruptions. This time, however, she could not resist replying. "Just wait a little while longer," she said in an aside that was clearly heard in the back row. "He becomes very nice in the next act."

In one scene she was required to pull a red bandanna out of her grandfather's pocket. The property man had forgotten to put one in, and when she reached for the kerchief, it was not there. "Well," she said resourcefully and without a pause, "I must have left it in my room. I'll just run and get it." To this day she is regarded as one of the best ad-libbers in the business. MacArthur once commented, "Helen puts me to shame with her spur-of-the-moment remarks. They're much better than the playwright's best lines."

When the company closed for the season, Mrs. Brown began to wheedle her husband into allowing the child to try to get a stage part in New York. She was sure that Helen was "ready for the big time." Every night for weeks she harangued him about "standing in the path of your daughter's certain fame!" Finally, Francis Brown realized that the only way he could ever get some peace was to buy two round-trip railroad tickets and promise that he would send $25 a week for their room and board—for a limited time.

Mother and daughter did not find New York show people ready to do headstands when they arrived. "We called at all the theatrical producers we ever heard of," Helen said sadly. "None of them were receptive. It was rejections all the way."

They were ready to use the return portion of their railroad tickets when Mrs. Brown recalled Lew Fields's offer. She had not gone to see him earlier because she felt that a "Dutch" comedian who wore a derby and loud checked clothes and was known for his dialect jokes was no proper appreciator of her daughter's talents. Now, holding Helen's hand, she called at the Weber and Fields office. They were kept waiting in the anteroom. After several hours the door to Fields's private office swung open. He emerged with glamorous Loretta Faust, a famous Broadway femme fatale, on his arm. He stared at the eager-looking pair, but there was obviously no sign of recognition. That was too much for Mrs. Brown. She grabbed her daughter, lifted her up, and said, "See this child? Do you remember—she's the one who impersonated Annabelle Whitford in Washington?"

Instead of telling her to get out of his way, Fields smiled. "Come right in!" he said.

That afternoon he signed Helen to play the part of Little Mimi in his fall production of the Victor Herbert operetta *Old Dutch*. Her salary would be $35 a week. "That was the most brilliant decision I ever made," he said. "Although there were other children in the cast, she stood out. She was with us for about four years in New York and on the road. In all that time she kept us on our best manners; we even took our hats off when she was present. We had to.

"Once when her mother was around—it seemed to us that Mrs. Brown was always around—I forgot to take my hat off and so did some of the other men. She stared at us like we were wearing bathing suits to go to see the Pope. Then she started this humming, 'H'm, h'm, h'm.' At first I didn't know what she meant. Then I realized it was because our hats were still on our heads. Helen guessed it right away and started giggling. As I took mine off, Mrs. Brown said in a hoity-toity way, 'Thank you for finally realizing that ladies require respect!'

"To tell the truth I really liked her," Fields added, "but I have to admit that she was a real stage mother if I ever saw one. She protected eight-year-old Helen something fierce. Nearly every grown-up female in the cast had a sugar daddy who'd regularly send her flowers and diamond bracelets. Even though little Helen was right in the middle of such goings-on, she probably was better safeguarded than some kid in Grand Rapids. Even her crush on Vernon Castle was babyish."

Castle had a leading role in *Old Dutch*. Although the famous ballroom dancer was many years older than Helen, he would play hide-and-seek backstage with her and endless games of jacks. Castle was not aware of her feelings until he announced that he was marrying actress Irene Foote and Helen burst out crying.

She remembers that first love. "When it happened, I felt it was the most wretched time of my entire life," she said. "My Prince Charming had left me for another woman. It's plain to see that I didn't have a very conventional childhood."

Helen and her mother returned temporarily to Washington. She was in her "awkward age"—too old for child parts, too young for more mature roles. However,

Mrs. Brown quickly arranged for Helen to be signed by a local group to play the young child in Elmer Rice's *On Trial*. She also enrolled her in another Washington Catholic school, the Sacred Heart Convent.

"They considered me some kind of celebrity," Helen said. "The other students and even the nuns begged me to tell them stories about the theatre. They often made me repeat them, but when they would choose up sides for their games, I was always left out. At the time I felt terrible. Now, I realize they thought I'd be bored by silly child games. Were they wrong!"

Alice Cahill, who was one of the first woman Red Cross ambulance drivers in World War I, was a senior at the time Helen attended the school. "Even though she wore a middy blouse like the rest of us," Ms. Cahill said, "we all knew she was Helen Hayes the actress. She seemed aloof. Distant. I know now that she was just shy. But still, she had mingled with famous people and had been to New York, Chicago, and Atlantic City, whereas the farthest I'd ever got at the time was to Mount Vernon. When she was in a play, her lessons would be sent in by the professional school. Things like that. I guess we were jealous. We called her 'stuck up.' "

Helen recalled, "I so wanted to be part of the group when I was in my early teens—to go to parties and balls, flirt from behind a fan, and fall deeply in love. I've never been so lonely and lost."

Mr. Brown hoped that Helen's acting days were over, that she and her mother had returned for good. Once more he tried to convince his wife that their daughter needed security. One day Helen came home from school to find her father in tears. Her mother, who had begun to drink heavily, was in the kitchen angrily slamming the icebox door. Helen knew there had just been a big fight.

Looking back, she realizes how mismatched her parents were. "I was the only thing they had in common," she said. "They were born antagonists, but I thank heaven for their misalliance. . . . My mother's dreams helped shape me. Her weakness made me strong. It taught me to accept responsibility."

"Helen was called upon," said a close friend, "to use the same understanding years later in her marriage to Charlie. She had good training for handling his drinking problem. A lesser wife would have fled, but the foreknowledge she had acquired from her mother helped sustain her."

Just as things in the Brown home were going from bad to worse a telegram from Broadway producer Charles Frohman arrived: "Bring your daughter to my office in the Empire Theatre building for an important part in a play with John Drew."

At the time Drew was the theatre's reigning star. His name assured producers and directors that their plays would receive maximum attention. "There's no modern-day actor that has Uncle John's influence," said Ethel Barrymore. "Even my brothers, Lionel and Jack, don't exert his onstage authority. He was truly in a class by himself."

Drew appreciated his own importance. "His ego," Frohman once said, "is so great that it towers high above the Alps!" He insisted on surrounding himself with the best possible talent. Mrs. Brown was thrilled that he even knew Helen existed, let alone wanted her for his play *The Prodigal Husband*. True, the play left a lot to be desired, but that made little difference to her. Helen's name would be on the same program as his. The Empire Theatre, which housed the show, was considered the jewel of Broadway. The calculating Mrs. Brown was not disappointed. On opening night she was happily dazzled by all the diamond tiaras surrounding her. In the course of the evening the audience gave her young daughter applause equal to Drew's. After the curtain came down for the final time, the great man said to her, "Now, Madam, take this child home to bed. Tomorrow, she too will be famous."

He was right. Although the critics felt that the play was not up to Drew's usual standards, they all agreed that Helen Hayes was a welcome addition to the theatre. Said one, "I venture to guess that a great deal more will be heard from this tiny, pixylike actress."

The Prodigal Husband, a very slight and sentimental comedy, was actually saved from shutting down only by the dynamic Drew. His name and charisma kept it running on Broadway for eight weeks. When it closed, Frohman took the entire cast on a series of one-night stands. The tour so exhausted him that he decided on a sea voyage to Europe. For passage on the return trip he selected the ill-fated *Lusitania,* which was sunk by a German submarine. Frohman drowned. Helen, who was to be fifteen the following October, sobbed to a reporter for the *New York Tribune,* "Charles Frohman was a dear man. He was so kind. He taught me so much. I'll never forget him."

Her grieving tribute to the late producer encouraged gossip. It was rumored that she was really the daughter of Frohman and his mistress, actress Maude Adams, whom Helen greatly resembled.

Years later, when Charles MacArthur learned about the rumor, he told Ben Hecht about it. "Now I know why Helen is so out of the ordinary. Having been created by two sets of parents, she belongs in Ripley's *Believe It or Not.*"

Helen said of her real father, Francis Brown, "He seemed always to be waving good-bye at the railroad station, getting smaller and smaller in my life, his brave smile blurring more and more as we chugged away. Still, in my memory, it is he who was there to comfort me."

When Helen was sixteen—and looked about eleven—she put up her hair, donned high heels, and applied for an ingenue part in Poli's Washington, D. C., Stock Company. The play, *Romance* by Ned Sheldon, did not require any young actresses. Mrs. Brown was against her daughter seeking the role. "They just won't believe you," she said. For one of the few times in her life, Helen defied her mother's wishes. "I was lonely," she said, "and paid no attention to her."

She got the part. On opening night she wore a sleek, pink evening gown. Mrs. Brown was right: she was not very convincing. The critics said so. However, since Helen had many fans in Washington, it was decided to give her another chance. Two weeks later she was again cast as a grown-up. In this role she was required to light and smoke a cigarette. "Helen practiced very hard," said her mother. "She held the cigarette as if she expected it to go off. Coughing and spitting, but still trying to act nonchalant and sophisticated. . . . It was just too much for the director, who, after three days of rehearsal, took the part away."

Mrs. Brown finally persuaded her daughter that she

was not quite ready for ingenue roles, that she would have to continue to play "fresh-faced youngsters" for several more years. When she learned that George Tyler, a well-known producer and agent, was casting a road company for *Pollyanna, the Glad Girl*, she decided that Helen would be perfect for the leading role. Tyler, who had brought Sarah Bernhardt to this country, was known to hire only top-notch talent. Helen was brought to see him. His first words were, "And here's my Pollyanna."

The critics approved of his choice. When the show opened in Rochester, one wrote, "Never before have I seen more perfect casting. Not only is Helen Hayes perfect for this role, but dozens of other roles."

Slowly, the play moved from coast to coast. The country's youngest leading lady received similar praise in most of the towns she performed in: "Tyler is a genius for having selected the whimsical Helen Hayes for the title role." "She plays with so much eloquence and genuineness that she has you believing she really *is* Pollyanna." "Helen Hayes may be young in years, but she is a veteran when it comes to talent. She knows every mannerism, every will-o'-the-wisp dream, every nuance in the acting book. The child is great, great, great."

Helen celebrated her seventeenth birthday in Fort Keogh, Montana. That afternoon a group of World War I soldiers who were about to embark for France brought her a birthday cake. A grizzled sergeant who had been selected as the spokesman said, "You make it all worthwhile. This is what we are going over there for—so wonderful children like you can continue to be!"

Tyler next brought Helen to New York, where he cast

her in Booth Tarkington's *Penrod* as the older sister. She was no longer required to play the youngest child in the show. That distinction fell to Ben Grauer, who later became a famous radio announcer. He said, "Even though Helen was older, she was still tinier than many of the kids in the cast. That didn't stop us from looking up to her. After all, she was a full-fledged actress. Many was the time she'd tell me what I was doing wrong. But she'd do it in such a way it almost sounded like a compliment. She's been my secret love for years."

Again the critics raved about Helen's performance: "Andrew Lawler, who plays Penrod, is good, but Penrod's older sister Margaret, played by Helen Hayes, is excellent."

The 1918 influenza epidemic closed *Penrod*, which had been housed at Broadway's Punch and Judy Theatre. The New York City Board of Health insisted that every play that children were likely to attend had to close until the scourge had passed.

Helen was not out of work for very long. A few days after the show was halted, she was signed for what turned out to be her biggest hit yet. She was to appear opposite William Gillette in Sir James M. Barrie's *Dear Brutus*. Dozens of major actresses sought the role, but Alfred Hayman, successor to Charles Frohman, felt that only Helen Hayes was right for the part. He said, "I desperately wanted to get someone equal to Mr. Gillette's ability—he was without a doubt the finest actor on the stage. I decided that Helen Hayes was it."

On November 11, 1918, the show was in rehearsal when work was suddenly interrupted by fire-engine sirens, church bells, and horns. Everyone dashed outside to investigate. They discovered that the armistice ending World War I had just been signed. Mrs. Brown grabbed her daughter's hand, and the two of them raced to Saint Patrick's Cathedral, which was ten blocks distant. On the way they passed the Knickerbocker Hotel, where a window on the second floor opened and Enrico Caruso, the opera star, put his head out and started singing "The Star-Spangled Banner." Helen said that she will remember his voice as long as she lives. "I still get goose bumps when I think of it."

Charlie loved to tell that story. However, his version was slightly different. He declared that "the reason for all Caruso's passion was that he was staring directly at Helen. He had seen her perform, and to him she symbolized what America stood for."

Helen's appearance in *Dear Brutus* greatly enhanced her theatrical reputation. Although offstage she still resembled a studious seventh-grader, at eighteen she had reached her full growth. "She is the teeniest big star on the stage," wrote a Boston critic. "Standing on her toes she is five feet plus a very thin slice of delectable crepe suzette. With her pockets filled with marbles she weighs in at a hundred pounds. Has a tipped-up nose and long, straggly blonde hair. But once she starts taking a role, she becomes a professional's professional. . . . There wasn't a dry eye in the house when she got through wringing out the scene where Gillette, the childless artist, meets the daughter he might have had."

Helen could now pick and choose her own roles. However, she continued to rely on her mother's judgment. When Mrs. Brown strongly suggested that she return to George Tyler, Helen did so. The following season she appeared with Alfred Lunt in the Tyler production of *Clarence*, in which she played Cora Wheeler, a young flapper. In costume, she wore above-the-knee dresses and projected her first sexy image.

"It's rare that a play's author pays tribute to an actor," said Tyler. "But that's exactly what Booth Tarkington did. After seeing her take twenty-five curtain calls on opening night, he told me that her performance of Cora didn't leave a look, gesture, or intimation that could possibly be imagined different. 'No actress in the world,' he said, 'except Helen Hayes could make that completely right, soul-satisfying portrait.'"

Alexander Woollcott, who was then the critic for *Everybody's* magazine said, "Her technique is so remarkable that older and more experienced actresses sit open-mouthed and wonder where and how she learned it. . . . Her vamp role so excited the opening night audience that they made confetti out of their programs and tossed them in the air." The "endowed extravert"—as Charlie often called Woollcott—added, "If they knew her in person, they'd soon find out that she's the most unflapperish girl around."

At the time, Helen was quietly in love with Lunt, her co-star. But as a properly brought-up young lady she could not admit it. She wept when she discovered that Lynn Fontanne was visiting his dressing room nightly. Her grief was lightened somewhat by the antics of a young sailor. Regularly, he would stand outside the stage door and toss rose petals at her feet when she exited. He stopped only after being seized by the Shore Patrol for being AWOL. She once said, "I wonder what would have happened if I had encouraged that sailor?"

After leaving *Clarence*, Helen played the ingenue in

Bab, which was based on stories by Mary Roberts Rinehart. Even though she was growing up she continued to
be "mama's little refined girl." Mrs. Brown still super-
vised her daily activities, selected her clothes, and carefully doled out an allowance for lunch. Helen did not
use the money for food. Every day before reporting for
rehearsal—she was allowed to go there by herself—she
would stop at a florist shop and buy a gardenia. She
would pin the white flower on her dress and hope the
other members of the cast would think it had been giv-
en to her by an admirer.

She finally got a bona fide boyfriend of her own
when *Bab* was booked in Boston for eleven weeks. During that time she became infatuated with a Harvard senior named Edgar. He wore a raccoon coat and bow ties
with polka dots, and he took her tea dancing. Naturally,
Mrs. Brown usually went along as a chaperon.

Helen was thrilled when her young beau published a
passionate poem in the *Harvard Lampoon* and dedicated
it to her. It reads in part:

> If man has considered Troy's
>   Helen perennial,
> As years and aeons go rollicking by,
> Let us hail our own Helen, the
>   millennial.
> If Broadway's the God that can give her
>   the glory,
> Her talents and charms are entitled to
>   win.
> Let Boston prefix "Chapter One" to the
>   story,

For Bab in her triumph—we saw it
  begin!
Good luck to you, Helen, when Fate will
  bereave us.
Of you and the coat sleeves that covered
  your paws,
You'll steal our poor hearts, precious
  burglar, and leave us
Alone in the echoes of Boston's applause.

Edgar's mother feared that her smitten son would el-
ope with the "precious burglar." Her concern disappeared when Mrs. Brown assured her, "I would object
to a marriage. My daughter would have so very much to
lose." Then, asserting her customary authority, she reminded her daughter that her acting would suffer if
she "plunged into a whirl" of gaiety.

Benchley had once called Helen "a gifted greasepaint
grind." Now, she worked harder than ever and seldom
strayed from Broadway. In rapid succession she appeared in *The Wren* by Booth Tarkington, *Golden Days*,
and *To the Ladies*, which George Kaufman and Marc
Connelly had written expressly for her.

"It was while I was appearing in *To the Ladies* at the
Maxine Elliot Theatre that it happened," Helen recalled. "I was walking along Fifth Avenue when I ran
into Marc Connelly. I helped him select a Christmas
present for his lady friend, Margalo Gilmore. Then he
asked me if I would accompany him to a party at a studio on Fifty-seventh Street. At first I was reluctant because although I was already an established actress, I
was leading a very secluded life. But I accepted. It was

the luckiest thing I ever did. There I met this beautiful young man who offered me some peanuts and murmured that he wished they were emeralds. From that moment on my life was changed forever."

3

The Princess Courts
the Prince

"**U**sually it's the man who is moved to do the wooing," said Marc Connelly. "In the case of Charlie and Helen the roles at the outset were reversed. I suppose I started it when I took her to Neysa's. Once he got off that now classic gallantry about peanuts and emeralds, she was enchanted—and promptly enslaved. I suppose it was natural—an actress falling for a perfect line by a fine writer."

Helen came to regret repeating that story. It was told and printed so many times that it drove MacArthur wild.

Charlie took her home from the Neysa McMein soiree in a hansom cab. Slowly, it moved down Park Avenue, where Helen shared an apartment with her mother and a girl friend.

MacArthur put a nonchalant arm around her shoulders and attempted to kiss her. She was startled. It was one of the few times that anyone had done that off the stage. Like the primly brought-up girl she was, she turned her head away. He grinned, pulled on his fore-lock, and turned his attention to the people in the street. Observing, in that fashionable neighborhood, women decked out in mink coats and men wearing homburg hats, he shouted, "Let 'em eat cake!" As the astonished pedestrians increased the pace, he added, "Make that cake topped with gobs of whipped cream!"

Although Donald Ogden Stewart said he knew it was love at first sight, it took Charlie several months to regard the affair as more than a casual flirtation. When he brought her home that very first time, Helen recalled, he saw her to the door, bowed, and said that he would soon call. She waited days and weeks, but no call. All she could do was think about him—how very dear and wonderful and brilliant he was.

Toward spring, Helen attended a party at Alexander Woollcott's home. One of the guests was Charles Mac-Arthur. She wanted to run up to him. Her Catholic-school training held her back. In her excitement she took a drink from a tray a butler was carrying and quickly downed it. "Lickety-split," said Connelly, "she had another. They were sweetly lethal concoctions Alec had invented called, naturally, Alexanders—lots of brandy and a goodly dash of sweet cream."

Fortified by the cocktails, Helen, who rarely touched liquor, announced giddily, "I'm moving to a new apartment. Anyone who wants my piano is willing to it."

George Kaufman, who was standing next to her, replied, "That's very seldom of you."

Everybody chuckled. The liquor, tinged with the laughter, gave the actress reckless courage. She danced over to Charlie and said breathlessly, "I'm opening in

Shaw's *Caesar and Cleopatra* at the new Guild Theatre. Why don't you come?"

"I'll try and catch your show," he answered politely.

The play was a respectable hit. Every night she would rush out on the stage before the performance began and look through the peephole in the curtain to see if he was in the audience. Helen Westley, a member of the cast, became aware of her agitation. She offered advice: "Call him and tell him to come!"

"I couldn't possibly do that," Helen replied. "It's not ladylike. Besides he might say no!"

Now that her secret was out, she pretended she was no longer interested in him but listened keenly to all the tantalizing tales about how Charlie MacArthur was rapidly becoming a legendary wit. How he and Bob Benchley had petitioned President Coolidge to make July 5 a national holiday "honoring flat-footed policemen." How he had told Alec Woollcott, "You must have been a three-letter man in college: *Me, Myself and I*." How he and Dotty Parker had been caught by federal agents in a Fifty-second Street speakeasy round-up.

Helen felt that she had little chance against such sophisticates and told herself she would probably never see him again. Then he walked into her dressing room one Saturday night in mid-July. She was so flustered that she stammered, "I . . . I . . . I'm very pleased to see you," she said. "I . . . I . . . I didn't know you were in the audience."

"I wasn't," he admitted truthfully. "I was just passing by and saw your picture in front of the . . ." He did not finish his sentence. Instead, his eyes were riveted on the bodice she was wearing. "It was a very flimsy black costume," she recalled. "I've never been more visible nor more transparent. His famous roving eye didn't move an inch."

Helen and her mother had taken a house for the summer in Syosset, Long Island. "Why don't you come out some weekend?" she asked MacArthur. Then very quickly she added, "Soon!"

"Tonight will be fine," he replied. "I'll drive to Syosset with you."

"That did it," said Stewart. "There were a great many stops and starts, but after that, Charlie was like a man in quicksand, caught but unable to believe it."

"My Charlie," Helen said, "became a regular weekend guest. He usually arrived without a suitcase— loaded down with nothing but a toothbrush and charm."

His winsomeness failed to capture Mrs. Brown. She said contemptuously, "He's a newspaperman! You know that means irresponsibility—and no money!" She tried to interest her daughter in more eligible men who were vacationing in Syosset. Paul Hammond, an avid yachtsman, was a steady caller. Another suitor of whom Mrs. Brown approved was a former ambassador. Helen wailed, "He's fifty-one years old!"

Helen was pleasant to them but made it clear that she preferred the company of madcap Charles MacArthur. Perhaps it was his devil-may-care attitude that endeared him to her. "All of my life I have worked hard to achieve success," she said to a friend. "Now, here comes a man who lives one happy-go-lucky day at a time and makes it work. And everybody loves him!"

Helen remembers that first summer as being full of

adventure. She felt that she was often out of her element, but with Charlie at her side she was secure. Together they visited his unpredictable friends who were holidaying in the area—the Herbert Bayard Swopes at Port Washington and Tommy Hitchcock at Great Neck.

Swope was the high priest of the Thanatosis Inside Straight Literary and Chowder Club, a poker-playing offshoot of the Algonquin Round Table. Helen did not know much about the game but she quickly realized that Charlie rarely held a winning hand. This did not stop him from betting. He loved to play. Winning, when he did, he was self-effacing and modest. Losing, he handed over blue chips or dollar bills with a careless air—"As though he was cleaning his feet on a boot scraper," said polo player Hitchcock.

Ben Hecht recalled that on the way to the noted horseman's summer home the couple had one of their first arguments. "By the time they pulled up to the front door, they weren't speaking," he said. "Charlie told me that when he walked across the threshold, he roared at Hitchcock, 'I'll wrestle you to the ground!' And then he dived right at his host."

For ten minutes the two opponents grimaced and grunted. Then suddenly MacArthur was flung through the air. He landed on his back with a loud thump. Helen crouched over his gasping, prostrate body. She began stroking his forehead and kissing him fervently. He opened his eyes and rubbed his sore back. "Is that the only way I can get your attention?" he asked.

"Neysa's country house was very much like her studio in the city," said Marc Connelly. "It was always filled with celebrities. You could usually find Charlie and Helen, Irving Berlin, Harpo Marx, Paul Robeson, Ring Lardner, and dozens of other people with well-known names. Word games were the order of the day. Somehow Charlie always won. I daresay he may have invented some of the words he stumped us with. But I will admit he was a walking dictionary and that most of his words were legitimate. At one game I remember, his word was *prothalamium*—it means 'bridechamber.' Helen looked at him with such adoration. As if it were the 'end all.' "

She was very anxious to show that she could appropriately entertain his witty companions. When he asked if Bob Benchley might visit for the weekend, she instantly said that she would be delighted to welcome him. Just before the humorist arrived, she gathered large bundles of Queen Anne's lace and goldenrod and tastefully decorated the foyer and living room. Benchley entered the house in his usual abashed manner; he behaved like a timid Fuller Brush salesman. In less than a minute his face turned purple. He began to sneeze violently. "Hay fever!" he shouted. He ran upstairs and barricaded himself in the guest room for his entire weekend. He stuffed sheets of newspaper in the cracks of the door. On departing, Benchley pecked the cheek of his distressed hostess and murmured, "I've never had such a restful time."

When Helen returned to New York in October she got an urgent call from Neysa McMein. "Beatrice Lillie is in from England," she said. "Bea wants to see you right away!"

Helen was frightened. Would Bea Lillie, international mistress of fast, funny lines and risqué jokes, reclaim Charlie, her former paramour? "I don't mind admitting," Helen said, "I was plain scared. Here was this great sophisticated lady and here I was, as complicated as bread and butter."

She changed her clothes about half a dozen times and literally had to force herself to leave the house. Helen said she was so self-conscious and afraid of Miss Lillie that she tried making wisecracks and shrieked at her own punch lines.

Bea Lillie saw through the performance immediately, realizing that Helen was terrified of losing Charlie. "Bea didn't have to say anything," Helen recalled. "She didn't have to tell me that Charlie was my property. I knew she had decided to keep hands off. I became a lifelong friend of this wonderful woman."

However, an arrangement between Helen and Mac-Arthur was far from being settled. Friends who cared for them both continued to be upset. Alec Woollcott phoned and asked if Helen would dine with him. On the ride to the restaurant, he was unusually silent. Suddenly, he spoke what he perceived to be painful truth. "Charlie," he said gravely, "is like quicksilver, not to be held onto. Helen, you can't possibly win." He was gloomier as the meal progressed. When the waitress finally handed him the check, he said, "Charlie will never be serious about anybody. To him you're just a pretty little stage-door fling!"

Margaret Case Harriman, the chronicler of the Algonquin Round Table, said, "Preventing any marriage from taking place always made Alec deliriously happy. Nothing bored him more than a couple's contentment. He did everything in his power to pull them apart. It didn't work with Charlie and Helen—they continued to be an obstinate item."

Woollcott was not alone in attacking Helen's marriage plans. She was told by a Roman Catholic bishop that being wed to a divorced man would mean certain excommunication from the church and she would run the risk of eternal damnation.

Charlie introduced her to his father. "You are a sinner!" thundered the reverend, who rejected all forms of commercial entertainment. "No son of mine will ever marry an actress!"

Mrs. Brown also tried to break up the romance. She saw in it neither prestige, money, nor happiness. Repeatedly, she found ways to point out to her daughter that Charlie was fickle. "A week after the honeymoon he'll leave you for another woman, mark my words!" she prophesied. "Before you know it, you'll be alone. There will be children! And then what will your career be?"

Helen tried to reassure her mother that unplanned children couldn't possibly happen to her. "We've agreed to wait," she said demurely.

"That's what I said when I married your father," Mrs. Brown said sadly. "Then look what happened!"

It seemed that the more contrary advice Helen received, the more certain she was that Charlie was the man for her. She defied her mother, the Reverend MacArthur, the Roman Catholic Church, Woollcott, and all the others.

Charlie was now quite certain: Helen would be the next Mrs. MacArthur. He tried to clear the way for matrimony by convincing Carol Frink, his estranged wife, to apply for a divorce. After filing the necessary papers, Carol abruptly changed her mind. "Even a distant husband," she said, "is better than none. Besides, Charlie may even become famous."

His lawyer advised him to make a financial arrangement with her and start a countersuit. All of this took time. Meanwhile, MacArthur wanted to be alone with Helen. The small apartment she shared with her ever-present mother was not the best meeting place. They would often have dinner at Child's, a dreary restaurant that was several blocks from her home.

"They'd hold hands, stare into each other's eyes and drink their coffee very slowly," recalled Amos Newcomb, a former busboy. "They'd stay until it came time for closing; we'd almost have to force them to leave. One time when I told Mr. MacArthur it was closing time and he and Miss Hayes had to clear out, he took out his wallet and offered me $3. I could plainly see it was all the money he had. He told me to take it and 'get lost.' I said, 'Okay, you can stay while I clean the tables and mop the floor.' I didn't count on the manager, who ordered them to leave at once. I felt real sorry and tried to return the $3. Mr. MacArthur refused. 'Keep it,' he said, waving his hand. 'Your attempt was noble. I can always tell a man of sterling character.' Then he walked out as if he was a king."

Sometimes when Child's shut down for the night, they would go to Alfred Lunt's brownstone. He and his wife, Lynn Fontanne, lived in a walkup that had dark and quiet landings, and there Helen and Charlie would lay in each other's arms on the stairs, kissing.

On Sundays, Charlie often took Helen to Nyack, where he had lived as a youngster. They went by train to Tarrytown and then crossed the Hudson River by

ferry. Helen remembers the trip as being very romantic. "An old man played the accordion," she said.
"Charlie would have lots of request numbers. When we
got to Nyack, we'd walk around town and then sit for
hours in Schmidt's Ice Cream Parlor on Main Street.
When it was cold, we drank hot chocolates."

Schmidt's Ice Cream Parlor offered eight flavors of
homemade ice cream. Charlie once ordered all eight
varieties and passed out spoonfulls to startled customers. Once, a group of young boys came into the store
and looked lovingly at the lavish sundaes set out on the
MacArthur table. They ordered small-sized cones.
Charlie intervened.

"Large sundaes for my young friends," he bellowed.
"The treat's on me." He paid the bill, but when it came
time to board the ferry, he had to borrow funds from
Helen—he had spent his last dollar on the boys.

During the summer, Charlie and Helen would be invited to Woollcott's home in Bomoseen Lake, Vermont.
It infuriated Alec that Mrs. Brown often tagged along.
"My disapproval of the marriage is one thing!" he
would say belligerently. "But I won't tolerate anyone
else's interference!"

He decided to aid the "sweetkins." Croquet was his
favorite game. He insisted that everyone present join
him. When it came his turn, he would viciously send
Mrs. Brown's ball careening down a steep hill. Labo-
riously, but sportingly, she would hike down to fetch it,
and it was as much as half an hour before she made the
climb back. "That will give Charlie and Helen time to
be together," he would say devilishly.

Helen was now appearing in *What Every Woman
Knows*, a period revival that earned her $500 a week.

Charlie, who called for her every evening at the Bijou Theatre, became an idol of Jerome Klein, a retarded eighteen-year-old who ran errands for the backstage crew. The boy worshipped "Miss Hayes' steady honey" and roared at everything he did and said. Klein was the butt of the other employees' jokes. They would wink knowingly as they told the boy they wanted him to purchase pigeon eggs, thirteen-inch rulers, and long-stemmed blue roses.

Charlie recognized the cruelty of arrogance and hated it. That is when he sent him out to buy several dozen boxes of strawberry Jello. Then he had the youth help him empty the contents into the toilet and wash-up sink the backstage workers used. Then the two plotters added hot water to the mix. After a while the gelatin firmed up. The startled employees never picked on Jerome Klein again.

Whenever Charlie and Helen were together, they discussed the future. Helen had the lead role in *Coquette*, a drama that was produced by Jed Harris. Noel Coward, the British writer known for his witty, brittle, and sophisticated comedies about the leisure class, did not often hand out compliments. After seeing *Coquette*, he said, "Helen Hayes gave an astonishingly perfect performance. . . . She ripped our emotions to shreds."

Although now a major star, Helen told Charlie that her dearest wish was to be a wife and mother. He said honestly that his dearest wish was to be the author of a hit Broadway play. His last one, *Salvation*, which he wrote with Sidney Howard, had failed to receive the rave reviews he had hoped for. It had showed promise, but not at the box office.

"Dame Fortune is about to smile," Charlie said. "I'm collaborating with Ben Hecht on a play about the newspaper business. It should work out pretty good." MacArthur had made a giant understatement. It was *The Front Page*, one of Broadway's greatest successes.

4

The *Front Page* Chronicle

Charlie told Helen that he could not marry until one of his plays was "really significant . . . you know what I mean, a play that changes things." In 1928 *The Front Page* made that mark.

MacArthur and his collaborator, Ben Hecht, drew from their experiences as reporters covering the Cook County Criminal Courts Building in Chicago. The pair wanted to show what life was really like in the city jails, where cynical journalists daily wait for news of the worst.

The play logged all the underhanded deals, tricks, and connivances that went on in those small, grubby press rooms. It portrayed what has since become a stereotype of the city reporter. He is tough, wisecracking, cocky. His battered fedora is never off his head; the angle at which he slants its brim denotes his mood. His feet are always on his desk, and his desk drawer is never without its pint. He is sentimental, generous, and utterly democratic, at ease anywhere with anyone. He is Charlie MacArthur.

In *The Front Page* he is called Hildy Johnson, a reporter who has fallen in love with a conventional-minded sweet young thing. She agrees to marry him only if he will move to New York City and take a respectable job in advertising. He has agreed, given notice, and is going. His fierce, opportunistic, unprincipled city editor, Walter Burns, has threatened, schemed, and bribed in an attempt to dissuade him. But to no avail. Sadly, and with his fingers crossed, Burns gives Hildy his last assignment—to cover the execution of Earl Williams, a white man who has killed a black policeman. The viewer is given to understand that if the shooting had occurred in a white neighborhood, little notice would have been taken, but the blacks control four valuable precincts and an election is coming up. In his desperation, Williams, a confused young radical, says that he is being persecuted as an "anarchist," a word that aroused intense feelings in a nation still arguing about the Sacco-Vanzetti execution of only two years earlier.

Lolling in the press room, Hildy is suddenly confronted by the murderer, who has escaped, and the condemned man's sweetheart, a prostitute who has helped him. Hildy abruptly stops dreaming of Madison Avenue and the respectable life. Here is a lifetime opportunity for a great news scoop. As pursuing footsteps and shouts are heard, Hildy hides the fugitive in a rolltop desk. Then he grabs the telephone and yells for his editor. Stop the presses! Examiner Captures Escaped Murderer!"

The door bursts open, and in rush the police, the mayor, the rival newsmen, Hildy's angry fiancée, her mother, a hoodlum, and the city editor. In the frantic action that follows, the prostitute jumps out a window to avoid betraying her lover; Hildy's mother-in-law-to-be is taken for a ride by the hoodlum; telephones ring shrilly; reporters holler and bawl; and in the background, like a Greek chorus, players in a perpetual poker game chant: "Raise you ten!" "I'm out." "Shuffle that deck."

A messenger from the governor's office brings a reprieve. Everyone is happy. The editor gives Hildy his gold watch. The newspapers go to press. Hildy, his fiancée, and her mother are reconciled, and Hildy promises again that he will go to New York and give up reporting forever.

Then as the curtain begins to descend, the city editor, alone in the littered press room, grabs the telephone. He is calling his own newspaper. "Hello, Duffy? Send a wire to the chief of police of La Porte, Indiana. Tell him to meet the 12:40 New York Central out of Chicago and arrest Hildy Johnson and bring him back here. . . . The son of a bitch stole my watch!"

The Front Page electrified theatregoers. The play had 276 performances on Broadway (a long run in those days) and has been revived on both sides of the Atlantic. Hollywood made three different film versions of it. Helen appeared in one of the stage revivals playing Mrs. Grant, the mother of Hildy's fiancée. The role was modeled after her own mother, she said. "At the time Charlie and I were courting, she was a thorn in his side. There's a line in the play where Hildy says, 'I have three tickets to New York for me, my girl and her goddamn ma.' That was Charlie speaking from his heart. Later, mother and Charlie became good friends, and she thought the play was great. I agreed with her. *The Front Page* was a modern classic!"

Woollcott said, "I don't believe many people realize the importance of *The Front Page*. The two geniuses who wrote that *magnum opus* literally turned Broadway around. It was a new kind of realism. After its opening night the theatre was never the same again. Thank God."

Tennessee Williams, one of the country's leading playwrights, agreed. *"The Front Page,"* he said, "took the corsets off the American theatre and made it possible for me to write my kind of a play."

Adolph Ochs, publisher of the *New York Times*, stood almost alone in his condemnation of the play. He indignantly considered it a libel of all newspaper publishers, particularly himself, and strenuously objected to the rough language. He was incensed by a line describing a reporter "as a cross between a bellboy and a whore." He also resented an actor portraying a newsman who once worked on the *Times* saying, "It was like working in a bank."

"The play was written mainly at our apartment on Beekman Place," recalled Mrs. Rose Cayler Hecht, Ben's widow. "The boys worked on it for over a year. They followed the same routine they did on all their collaborating: Ben would have a pencil, paper, and lapboard. Charlie would amble around the room, lie down on the couch, draw beards on the girls on magazine covers. Some days they didn't write more than a couple of lines, but when it came time for them to write 'thirty,' they had finished a work of art. Although, I must admit that I liked their first play, *The Moonshooter*, much better. Sadly, it was never staged because the boys got

drunk and lost the manuscript. They were forever doing things like that.

"Once they were struggling for just the right lines for
Walter Burns, the tough city editor. After a long tussle,
they got it just right: 'Hildy, hit 'em where it hurts.
Right in the breadbasket. And I'm being polite when I
say breadbasket.' They went out to the corner pub to
celebrate. Along the way they lost the paper containing
the dialogue. It never did appear in the play."

One of the scenes they reluctantly left out of *The
Front Page* concerned an actual experience Charlie had
had in Chicago. "We had tried it and tried it," explained Hecht. "It was superb, but somehow we just
couldn't make it come off."

When he was reporter for the *Herald-Examiner*, Mac-
Arthur had covered a story involving Lieutenant Carl
Wanderer, a World War I hero who was charged with
murdering his wife. Although Charlie had played a
role in catching Wanderer, the lieutenant had taken a
shine to the young newsman. When MacArthur lent
the condemned man $5 for a poker game, Wanderer
asked if there was anything he could do for Charlie.

"Yes," MacArthur answered quickly. "Just before
you step off the platform you'll be asked if you have
any last words. Let me write out a speech for you."

"I'm not good at memorizing," the lieutenant complained.

"You can read it," Charlie assured him. He then composed a dolorous tirade that Wanderer was to deliver
just before he want to his death; it was a derisive attack
on the *Herald-Examiner* editor. Unfortunately, the type-
written paper that Charlie had given him slipped from
his hands and rolled out of reach as he made his final

walk. He looked sadly at MacArthur and instead sang "Dear Old Pal O' Mine."

When writing, Charlie eagerly welcomed every possible distraction—the constant ringing of the telephone, all-night drinking parties, fetching Helen from *Coquette* at Broadway's Maxine Elliott Theatre. "Sometimes he would be so tanked-up," recalled one of the ushers, "that he'd reel about at a forty-five degree angle. But even then he'd joke around with us. I don't believe anyone of us had a mean word to say about him. How could you? That guy was always a pure joy."

On weekends Charlie especially welcomed interruptions of anything he was supposed to be doing. Most of his escapades are memorable. He was once abruptly invited by Otto Kahn to a formal party at the financier's Long Island estate. MacArthur arrived wearing a properly fitted dinner jacket, black pants with a narrow satin stripe, freshly pleated shirt, black silk bow tie—and white tennis sneakers. He had forgotten to put on his black patent leather shoes. Hastily, Kahn found him a pair, but they were several sizes too small.

"You've got to wear them!" Kahn insisted. "Squeeze into them!"

Charlie painfully complied but felt that he had to retaliate. Shortly after dinner he closeted himself in the financier's library. He removed a half dozen leatherbound volumes from the shelves. On the fly leaves of each book he carefully wrote, "To my great friend and patron, Otto Kahn, without whose help this would never have been written." Then with a flourish he signed the authors' names—Voltaire, Balzac, Plutarch.

Another unforgettable incident occurred at Herbert Bayard Swope's Manhattan town house. One Saturday night Charlie and his fellow members of the Thanatosis Inside Straight Literary and Chowder Club were engaged in some serious poker-playing in an upstairs back parlor. MacArthur had a seven of diamonds showing a two of clubs as his closed card. He decided that the time was ripe for a good bluff. Short of money, he wrote out a deed to the rights of "my next play." Swope witnessed it.

On the next go-around Charlie drew a five of clubs. This time he bet "all the future rights to my second-from-now play." This document was certified by Harpo Marx. His next card was a nine of spades. Alec Woollcott signed the deposition for "rights from my third-from-now-play." MacArthur drew his last card, an eight of hearts. He once again made an extravagant wager—"rights from my fourth-from-now play." Benchley signed the statement. Everybody remained expectantly in the pot. Charlie said, "I had visions of bending eternally over a hot typewriter that forever dissolved in steam. Then the players showed their closed cards. They had a potpourri of nothing—my nine of spades was victorious!"

During the writing of *The Front Page*, MacArthur was often without funds. Helen was on a road tour. There was no one to restrain the opportunistic use of his charm and ingenuity. "There's been a rash of midtown robberies," he confided to a friend. As planned, word got back to Mary Harriman Rumsey, Averell Harriman's sister, who lived in the area. She begged him to move into her house on East Fortieth Street while she was traveling in Europe. He did so. He took care of his meals by dining regularly at opulent parties. "So many," he said, "that I fear I put on weight. Maybe, I

didn't have big money, but I sure acquired a big belly!"

Charlie's drinking was overseen by his legion of
companions. Traffic cops, bootleggers, polo players,
musicians, reporters, editors, and poets were all pleased
to sit beside him and thoughtfully refill his glass.
"Sometimes," said Hecht, "he showed up so pie-eyed I
didn't think he could possibly write a line. But not only
did he work, he was brilliant. Finally, with enough
schnapps behind us, we finished the play.

"As authors we didn't know which name to list first,"
Hecht added. "Charlie suggested we toss a coin. I remember he said he'd flip it so there wouldn't be any
cheating. He did and called heads. It came out tails."

Jed Harris, a young, ambitious, and keenly perceptive producer, immediately recognized the play's excel-
lence. "It's teacup gin," he said. He agreed to produce it
and hired George S. Kaufman as director. Rehearsals
began at once.

Hecht had to make a quick trip to Hollywood to write
the scenario for a movie for Metro-Goldwyn-Mayer.
Just before he departed, he grabbed Charlie and said,
"Don't let them rewrite the basics. Don't let them
change the heat of this!"

"Right off George Kaufman, the director, started
wondering about the rolltop desk that the murderer
was hiding in," said Frances Fuller, who had the part of
Hildy's sweetheart. "Charlie treated George's uncer-
tainty with the proper amount of respect. With a
straight face he said, 'Boss, what do you think of making the murderer a midget? In that way we can hide
him in a wastebasket.' George turned white. But Charlie wasn't quite finished. 'Better still,' he said, "maybe

he could be cast as a very tiny midget, and we could stash him in the cuspidor.' At the last suggestion George replied resignedly, 'All right. All right. I know when I'm licked. Let's get on with the rehearsal and keep that damned rolltop desk!' "

Harris was also the producer of *Coquette*. He closed it for one night on August 14, 1928, so that Helen could attend the opening performance of Charlie's play. Richard Maney, the publicist for both shows, recalled, "Helen was in a steady-running hit, but she believed Charlie when he said he would never ask her to marry him unless he, too, had a theatrical triumph. She went to the Times Square Theatre with her fingers crossed and a prayer in her heart. I remember she sat alone in the balcony near the fire exit. Charlie and Ben had chosen to sit on the fire escape, and she wanted to be close by to report the reaction of the audience.

"From the moment one of the card players in the opening scene spoke his first line, 'Crack it for a dime,' she knew Charlie and Ben had a hit. The audience roared. They applauded wildly. They stamped their feet. They whistled. I've never heard such carryings on. Charlie Chaplin was sitting up front. The comedian said he had nearly wet his trousers from so much laughing. After the final curtain Helen rushed out to announce that Jed felt the play would probably run forever. Charlie put a finger on her lips, braced himself on the iron railing, and asked, 'Helen, will you marry me?' " She promptly accepted.

Maney said that on the way out of the theatre, she ran into Tallulah Bankhead. Helen maneuvered the outspoken, worldly actress into a corner. "There's a very intimate question I'd like to ask you," Helen whispered.

She gulped several times as she carefully made sure no one else was listening. When she was satisfied they could not be overheard, she stammered, "When a girl gets married, what can she do to keep from getting pregnant?" Tallulah stared at her friend and then said throatily, "Just what you've always been doing, darling!"

The following morning Helen and Charlie "secretly" rushed to City Hall where they filled out a marriage application:

WEDDING CERTIFICATE NO. 20374

From the bride:

      Helen Brown

Color: White

Residence: 15 Park Avenue, NYC

Place of birth: Wash., D.C.

Age: 27

Occupation: Actress

Name of father: Francis V.

Maiden name of mother: Catherine Hayes

Number of marriages: First

From the groom:

      Charles MacArthur

Color: White

Residence: 152 East 40th Street, NYC

Age: 31

Occupaton: Writer

Place of birth: Scranton, Pa.

Name of father: William

Maiden name of mother: Georgiana Welstead

Number of marriages: Second

Divorced: Yes, June 26, Chicago, Ill.

Charlie and Helen had decided on a very quiet ceremony to forestall Charlie's ex-wife from stirring up more trouble. She was already claiming that the divorce was fraudulent and threatened to get out an injunction to prevent his marrying again.

MacArthur was put in touch with a former city magistrate who promised that he would marry the couple "with great dignity and without the slightest publicity." Charlie hired a limousine and with Helen, her mother, and Alexander Woollcott, who was to serve as the best man, drove to the judge's office on Forty-second Street. They were ushered in by a secretary and told to sit down. She said the judge was in the men's room. After waiting for forty-five minutes, they complained about the delay. The judge finally made an appearance and began chatting and puttering about. He showed them a photo of his four-year-old granddaughter. "Doesn't she look like another Helen Hayes?" he asked.

Then, still stalling, he said, "I want you to cast your eyes at something I'm thinking of investing in." He opened the top drawer of his desk and took out a hard-boiled egg, a piece of whole-wheat bread, and a miniature pickle. "Would you believe they're all made of soap?" he inquired. "I'll bet I make a million!"

He was about to enlarge upon the venture when his secretary burst in and shouted, "You can go ahead with the ceremony! The press is here!"

A very angry MacArthur threatened to punch the judge in the nose. The bride's mother kept shaking her head as if to say, "Didn't I warn you?" The best man said, "Every woman should once in her life be married to Charles MacArthur."

The ceremony, when finally under way, was indeed

brief—less than two minutes. After a wedding supper of lobster diable at Ben Hecht's apartment, the bride, who was still appearing in *Coquette*, hurried to the theatre to get ready for her performance.

As the curtain went up, a newsboy who was standing in front of the building, hawked his papers. "Read all about the secret wedding of Helen Hayes and Charles MacArthur!" he yelled. "Is he a bridegroom or a bigamist?"

5

The Royal Family of Broadway

Walter Winchell, who at the time of the nuptials was writing a gossip column for the *New York Evening Graphic*, said, "Front Page Charlie MacArthur and his brand-new bride Coquette Helen Hayes (not really!!!) have overnight become the royal family of Stagedom. Every noosepaper in the country is suddenly running heady tales about those two celebs who are now the most sought after sovereigns along the White Way."

In the days following the wedding Charlie and Helen received dozens of invitations to formal dinners, weekends, elegant lunches, studiedly decadent brawls, church functions. "Everybody, but everybody, was dying to gawk at this diverse pair," said George S. Kaufman. "They treated the curious alliance just as if President Calvin Coolidge decided to become a vaudeville hoofer and had chosen Fanny Brice for his dancing partner. I fear that for most people Charlie being married to Helen was equally bizarre."

In the early months of their marriage the MacArthurs lived in a hotel. Charlie felt that it would be too strenuous for Helen to keep house and also appear nightly on the stage. He protectively accompanied her to and from the theatre. "It was an easy life," Helen recalled. "Someone else did the cooking. A maid changed our bed daily. Porters even carried our luggage. I rarely had to lift a finger."

She amused herself by coaxing the chambermaids to repeat her new name. " 'Mrs. MacArthur, may we make up your rooms?' was such sweet music," Helen said. "I'd pretend not to hear them, and they'd say the 'Mrs. MacArthur' part over and over. It got to be a game."

On weekends, the MacArthurs often visited Arden House in Harriman, New York. The lavish seven-thousand-acre estate was built by Averell Harriman's railroad-magnate father. It consisted of about a hundred rooms; it was so large that there was no accurate count. Averell closed most of the place and lived in the east wing.

Once when Charlie appeared late for dinner, he apologized by saying, "I was busy counting the rooms and got lost on the southwest stairwell. I promise it won't happen again. After this experience, I'll always bring a map along."

Woollcott, another visitor, agreed that carrying a map might be a good idea. He suggested that Arden House be turned into a home for indigent writers who suddenly run out of words. "Like Ben Hecht," he said, "for example."

Hecht, who was sitting opposite him, responded, "That is something that could never happen to you. Your gift of gab will flow until Niagara falls!"

The two adversaries continued to exchange insults. Charlie interceded. He looked at both men and said, "You just gave me an idea for the first scene of my next masterpiece! It will be cast in the deepest part of Hades. The stage will be filled with burning fires and smoking pits. Two characters closely resembling Alec and Ben meet. They talk to each other, but neither pays attention to what the other is saying. This goes on and on. Finally, the devil appears and thunders, 'I have just decided your punishment—you will have to listen to each other for eternity.' Curtain."

Sunday mornings in New York City were reserved for croquet matches in Central Park. Woollcott required all Round Tablers to participate. Stakes were $10 a wicket. Alec insisted on winning. He told the other players that his doctor had advised him that losing would be injurious to his health and was infuriated by MacArthur's inevitable "Charge it!" When Charlie's losses rose to $100 he gallantly offered to settle with Woollcott for "half a chocolate bar." Helen, who was quickly learning his style of repartee, added sweetly, "And half a stick of chewing gum."

Alec would shake his head and mumble, "What can you expect? Like husband, like wife!"

Helen felt that Woollcott had given her the greatest compliment—she loved to be closely identified with Charlie. She drew the line, however, when they visited speakeasies. Waiters assumed that Mrs. MacArthur would join Mr. MacArthur. She refused the highballs and instead ordered ginger ale. Alcohol was responsible for most of the newlyweds' arguments. Helen tried resolutely to overlook Charlie's constant drinking. She knew from experience with her mother that it did no good to nag or to plead or to shout, "Stop!" As a wife, however, she suddenly found the old problem painful and threatening.

It was very difficult, she said, to stand by and watch your husband destroy himself, but she quickly dismissed the idea of leaving him. After one fight so bitter that both were appalled, she said, "You'll have to shoot me to get rid of me!"

He would often do his drinking at Tony's, a famous speakeasy that was a favorite of literary and theatrical celebrities. Tony's, like all such establishments of the time, had a peephole in the door in order to distinguish customers from detectives. On one occasion, Charlie felt that the bouncer, who was handling the door, was rude to some guests. After a heated argument, the party was admitted, but one of MacArthur's friends was still very agitated. That's when Charlie assured him, "I'll take care of everything!"

He excused himself and ran to the nearest grocery store, where he purchased a very overripe orange and bit off the top. Then he returned and knocked on the door. When the peephole opened, MacArthur squeezed the orange violently. The juice squirted through the hole and splattered into the bouncer's eye. Charlie's guests never had trouble again.

Once inside Tony's, it was MacArthur's habit to request a corner table and sit with his back to the wall. "It's safer," a Chicago gangster friend had assured him. "You'll be able to always see anyone out to gun you down!"

Always, Charlie found it necessary to be the last one to leave any party. "That came from his Algonquin days," Helen explained. "He used to say that the moment one of the regulars left the Round Table, the remaining diners would start ripping him apart."

One night Jascha Heifetz, the violinist, gave a costume party. The invitation read, "Come as your real self." The MacArthurs arrived early. Helen was in a schoolgirl uniform. Charlie came dressed as a Paris taxi driver. He was in rare form and high good humor. After all the other guests had departed, he still showed no signs of going home. As the sun rose, Heifetz, the host, put on his own overcoat and started to walk out, saying, "I'm all confused. I thought this was my house. I guess it's your house. Good night, I had a wonderful time."

Several weeks after the wedding, Helen managed to get some time off from *Coquette*. She and Charlie decided that their delayed honeymoon should be a very restful one. They planned on a leisurely cruise to Bermuda. However, it was anything but tranquil. On shipboard they met another young couple, a Mr. and Mrs. Jack Conway. The foursome hit it off. They had beef tea, cocktails, and dinner together. They became such good friends that they decided to stay at the same hotel when they reached Bermuda. A short while after they checked in, there was a frantic knock on the MacArthurs' door. A hysterical Mrs. Conway shrieked that her husband had just collapsed and died.

Local authorities suspected foul play and insisted on an inquest. Charlie and Helen were ordered to testify. For the next three days they made numerous appearances before the police. Although the coroner finally determined that the cause of death was heart disease, the MacArthurs returned to New York in a very subdued mood.

Helen went on tour with *Coquette*. She felt she had to continue working to support her mother and father adequately. "Going away and leaving Charlie," she said sadly, "grew more and more difficult. I hated to be away from him."

During her absence MacArthur spent a great deal of time tippling with his friends. "He came to our house often," recalled Ben Hecht. "It was not uncommon that my wife, Rose, would complain that we drank our dinner. Between sips Charlie would jump up and telephone Helen, his speech becoming more slurred and emotional with every call. He was just like a lost little lamb."

In Boston, Helen was hospitalized for an ailment that had long plagued her: she was, and remains, allergic to theatre dust. Charlie rushed to her side. Common house dust caused her discomfort, too, but she could have her residence thoroughly scrubbed. It was virtually impossible to rid any theatre of the offender. MacArthur tried to forbid his wife to continue acting. She vetoed the suggestion and learned to control her sneezing and wheezing. "I flare my nostrils as I coast through a sentence," she explained.

Willpower and muscle manipulation did not always work. During one matinee she felt an unstoppable sneeze coming on. The explosion was a violent one. Always the trouper, she quickly apologized to Eliot Cabot, who was appearing opposite her. "There are so many of these wicked colds going around," she ad-libbed regretfully. "I guess I've caught one. Don't let me pass it on to you." She took three steps backward and picked up her lines.

A few days later, when Helen was playing bridge

with some of the other performers, the phone rang. It was Charlie. He said excitedly that he had just put down a deposit on an apartment. Several hours later he phoned again. "I've just located an even better apartment," he shouted gleefully. "I had to put a deposit on it."

"What about the first deposit?" Helen asked.

"Oh, that!" he said contemptuously. "This place is so superior. It's well worth losing a deposit."

The next few days he made three similar calls. "You are just tossing our money away like paper-the-house tickets," Helen moaned.

Actress Una Merkel, who was in the cast of *Coquette*, overheard the conversation, and when the exasperated Mrs. MacArthur put the receiver down, she said, "Just be glad he's only renting and not buying a home!"

Miss Merkel's consolation had been premature. The following afternoon Charlie telephoned again. "I just found exactly the right apartment. I had to buy it. The back window faces the East River, and you know how much you like looking at water."

MacArthur had purchased a cooperative apartment— a new idea in those days—on New York's posh East End Avenue. "It's only money," he told Hecht. "After all we're making plenty of it!"

He was quite right. *The Front Page* continued to play to standing room only. "We were the recipients of sizable weekly sums," said Hecht. "And we became even richer when Howard Hughes bought the film rights."

Jed Harris had cleverly maneuvered the sale. "One late night in January of 1929," said *The Front Page* producer, "I got a call from an unfamiliar voice. 'This is Ha'wd Hughes,' it said. Then Hughes made some small talk, asking if I knew of a play that might be a suitable vehicle for a female actress he wanted to help. We talked about that for a minute and then he said, 'By the way, you've got some kind of show running about the newspaper business. Its name just slipped my mind. Are the picture rights for sale?' "

Jed shrewdly thought it extremely unlikely that the name "just slipped" his mind. *The Front Page* was then the biggest hit on Broadway. "Hughes offered $50,000," Harris said. "At the time that was a pretty sizable price."

When he told Charlie and Ben about the offer, they chorused, "Grab it!" They were dismayed when the producer tried to assure them that he was certain he could get lots more money from Hughes. There was a great deal of discussion. "Don't tempt fate," Ben cautioned.

"Okay, we'll wait," Charlie said. "But don't be too greedy a son of a bitch. Don't take too many chances!"

The next week MacArthur and Hecht made daily visits to the Harris office. They wanted to know if there were any new developments. On the seventh day Jed said that he had just heard again from Hughes, who made his "last and final offer—$75,000."

Again, Jed strongly advised them not to accept. Fearfully, they allowed Harris to continue dickering. The following Thursday, Hughes raised his "last and final offer" to $100,000. Before Jed could check with Charlie and Ben, Hughes came back with another "last and final offer." This one was for $125,000. Jed agreed. MacArthur and Hecht were delighted, but a few minutes later Charlie said, "Do you suppose if we held out a little longer we could have gotten $150,000?"

Now that Helen and Charlie had a place of their own and plenty of money, they decided it was time to start a family. Helen traveled to New York from the road—wherever she was—to spend Sundays with her husband. "Our Mary was conceived right there," she said referring to their new East End Avenue apartment.

6
The Act-of-God Baby

In July 1929, Helen discovered that she was preg-nant. She did not at once seek professional care. "I was anxious to keep the news to Charlie and myself," she said. "It was our private joy. I wanted it to stay that way as long as possible."

When she was three months along, *Coquette,* which was still on tour, moved to Los Angeles. MacArthur started commuting regularly to the West Coast. It was cruelly exhausting in the days before regular air travel. He wanted to be near his wife and began writing movie scripts. They rented a bungalow in Hollywood. "Char-lie was the comic epitome of the soliticious father-to-be," Helen said. "He wanted to be at my side all the time."

One night at Pickfair, the awe-inspiring home of Douglas Fairbanks and Mary Pickford, Helen decided to show off before Maurice Chevalier, one of the guests. As the French singer tossed pennies into the swimming pool, she dived after them.

MacArthur was furious when he found out, insisting that she might have injured herself and the baby. Eventually, he calmed down, Helen recalled.

"You were foolhardy," he reprimanded her. Then he grinned and added, "At least you could have dived for quarters."

Helen kept her pregnancy secret from her mother. Mrs. Brown, who was still supervising her daughter's career, had also come to California. Helen had found her an apartment in Los Angeles. The MacArthurs often visited. One afternoon, just before they sat down for lunch, Helen fainted. An alarmed Charlie called a doctor, who ordered her to bed. "If you want to save the baby," he warned, "you'll stay there!"

Charlie immediately phoned Jed Harris and told him what had happened. Jed decided to close the show rather than replace his star with another actress. Members of the cast claimed that severance pay was due them by terms of the contract. Harris's lawyer pointed to a clause which said that actors are not entitled to salaries "if the company cannot perform because of fire, accident, strikes, riot, *act of God*" and so on. Both sides agreed the dispute should be arbitrated by the Actors Equity Association.

The newspapers latched onto the story. Many erroneously indicated that it was Helen Hayes who maintained that her pregnancy was an act of God. "Here I wanted to keep the news of the baby private," she said. "Suddenly, there was an avalanche of publicity. But Charlie—dear Charlie—managed to protect me from all the turmoil. He would meet the reporters on the front lawn. If I was looking out the window, he'd assure me he was just talking to some of the neighbors."

Helen remained in bed for more than two months before she was permitted to lead a near-normal life. "However," she said, "the doctor cautioned me to be very careful."

The night after the medical reprieve, Helen insisted on accepting an invitation to a dinner party. The MacArthurs' appearance coincided with a report that the afternoon newspapers carried about the Equity decision. Equity had ruled against Jed Harris. He was required to pay the actors for two additional weeks.

The guests were discussing the settlement. Donald Ogden Stewart said to Helen as he passed a tray of salted radishes, "I see you just made the funnies." Then he handed her a cartoon that featured a self-satisfied-looking stork sitting on a pile of money. Underneath the drawing the artist had written: "MacArthur baby not an act of God."

Charlie appeared coolly amused. "At long last," he said quite happily, "I'm getting a little credit for having something to do with it."

Irving Thalberg, MGM's "resident genius," wanted MacArthur to write the screenplay for a motion picture he was going to produce. It was to be titled *Rasputin and the Empress,* a movie about the Russian czarina and the mesmeric monk who may or may not have been her lover; history and the projected movie left the question up for grabs. Thalberg had obtained the services of Ethel, Lionel, and John Barrymore.

"It's rare," he proudly told Charlie, "to get them all together. Everyone's been trying."

"I'm not interested," MacArthur said.

"I can't get him to budge," Thalberg sadly told Ethel

Barrymore, who was to be cast as the empress. "He's the best scenario writer in the business."

"I'll bet I can!" she said. She stormed out of the plush office and drove to the MacArthurs' house. She did not bother to ring the bell. She simply barged in, grabbed Charlie by the shoulders, and shook him. "You're nothing but a lazy, good-for-nothing lout," she shouted. "You're going to write *Rasputin!* Or else!"

A very startled MacArthur managed to break away. He hid behind his wife, who had come in from the bedroom to see what all the commotion was about. "Charlie," she said, "no woman has ever talked to you like that. Do something!"

Before he could reply, Ethel kicked him in the shins and knocked some books off a table. "That's only the beginning!" she bellowed. "Unless you agree immediately, I promise I'll wreck both you and this house!"

"Charlie!" Helen wailed. "I don't think she's kidding!"

MacArthur backed down. "All right," he said weakly. "I'll do your damn picture. What's it about?"

Ethel Barrymore called Thalberg, who arrived at once. Together, they told Charlie all about the Romanovs and the mad monk. He typed wildly as they spoke. When they finished, he gasped, "I think I've got it . . . this simple, trusting religious man. . . ."

Ethel Barrymore broke in, "Remember, he's evil."

MacArthur ignored her and continued. "He's conned by the sexy, conniving, but politically wise dame," he said. "Finally, Rasputin conquers her. His mad sexual powers sold as religion—they both forget God and come to grief!"

Aside from Ethel's temper, Charlie's most formidable

problem was convincing the Barrymores that he was not favoring one of the others with choice dialogue. "One late afternoon," said MacArthur, "a furtive Lionel slipped away from the set to call at my office. I met him in the studio alley. 'That so-and-so brother of mine,' he said, 'is getting too smart. He's doing all sorts of treacherous things behind my back to steal a scene. What do you think he did today? I caught him red-handed wiggling his ears, pursing his lips, flicking dust from his larcenous backside, and stealing the whole scene from me. You've got to see to it that he quits this nefarious practice. Appeal to his better side—if you can locate it.' "

Charlie's solution was to send Lionel and John each a case of scotch. To Ethel, he had a florist deliver several dozen roses. Accompanying the gifts were carefully handwritten cards: "To my favorite Barrymore, CM."

When Helen was six months pregnant she and her mother returned to New York. Mrs. Brown, who still occupied the Park Avenue apartment, moved in with her daughter. Charlie had to remain in Hollywood to finish the script. He telephoned his wife and her doctor Ralph Lobenstine, several times a day to find out whether she was healthy. "Doc," he'd say, "take good care of the little mother. If you don't, I promise I'll come to your office and paint naked ladies on your chest!"

MacArthur made elaborate plans to rejoin his wife as soon as the script was completed. Moments after he finished the last page his colleagues threw him a farewell party. Several hours later an exuberant group of drunks waved merrily as they saw him off. Unfortunately, instead of putting Charlie on the train, they deposited him on a ship that was headed for New York via the Panama Canal.

Charlie said he did not realize the mistake until the vessel made a stop in Havana. He dashed off to call Helen. "The line was busy," he explained. "When I got back to the dock, I found they had sailed without me."

He spent the last money in his pocket to get as far as Florida, where he got in touch with Anita Loos, a close friend. He borrowed railroad fare from her and took the next train to New York's Penn Station, where Helen met him. He stepped off wearing a white T-shirt, white flannel trousers, and white tennis shoes. It was the middle of January, and there was snow on the ground. Helen with resigned foresight had brought along his overcoat and galoshes.

As the time of the birth drew near, Charlie became more and more concerned. "Doesn't a baby need lots of room?" he asked worriedly. That afternoon he bought an additional apartment in their East End Avenue building. "That's so she can get away from us when she wants to—no being tied to apron strings for our daughter."

"He desperately wanted a female child," Helen said. " 'Please make it a girl,' he'd plead with me. 'I don't want any so-and-so giving me competition.' "

No sooner had MacArthur purchased the extra apartment than he bought the yet-unborn child a full-sized billiard table. "It was so big," Helen said, "that it had to be hoisted through a window."

Charlie justified the expenditure by explaining it was a necessary adjunct to the child's growth and progress.

"The baby can learn to walk by hanging on the sides," he said.

That night the MacArthurs were summoned to the hotel suite of Grand Duchess Marie of Russia, who had arrived from Paris. Charlie had met Her Highness several years before at a party. Like most people, she was captivated by her "*darogoi krassvee drook*" (dear, beautiful friend). Helen felt that fast-approaching motherhood made her much too ungainly to meet royalty, but MacArthur cajoled her into going. "I assure you," he said, "even duchesses know all about pregnancy."

An imposing seven-foot butler ushered them into a crystal, gold, and mahogany drawing room. "It's all on the cuff," Charlie whispered. He was right. Sadly, the sumptuous suite was all that the duchess had been able to command. When it came time for dinner, it was painfully obvious that the royal lady had no cash and was denied charge privileges. Helen invited her to the East End Avenue apartment. She eagerly accepted. There, in the kitchen, Charlie, his wife, and Grand Duchess Marie of Russia ate scrambled eggs and swapped anecdotes about childbirth.

The evening before the infant's arrival the MacArthurs visited Ned Sheldon. The bedridden playwright wanted to know what they planned on calling the baby. Helen replied that they had not decided upon a name. "Charlie," she said, "feels that it has to be a girl. I guess we need feminine names."

"There's no prettier name for a girl than Mary," Ned said.

A few hours after they returned to their apartment Helen reported labor pains. MacArthur began fretting. He wanted to call the police or the fire department. His wife was very calm. She insisted on walking to the hospital, which was eight blocks away.

"Nothing much can happen," she said comfortingly.

Charlie paced a short distance behind his wife, murmuring "If anything happens here on the street, I'll pretend I don't know you!"

They reached the hospital in good time. Mary was born the morning of February 15, 1930. Astonished when shown his new daughter, Charlie said "Why, she's more beautiful than the Brooklyn Bridge!"

A short while later he took a longer look at the infant. This time, quite sober, he said reflectively, "Helen, we have given her birth and death. But that's about all we can really give her."

Helen knew it was true. "Life would shape her," Helen said. "Not her parents."

Soon after Mary was born, the hospital lobby was crammed with photographers and reporters. They all hoped to see the "act-of-God baby." After checking with the MacArthurs, Dr. Lobenstine grudgingly consented to allow pictures of the one-day-old infant in order to clear the place of the press. When the reporters finally left a dark-eyed young woman remained seated in the corner. She was very pregnant.

"I must see Helen Hayes," she told a nurse in a soft but desperate voice. "I won't leave until I do!"

After a great deal of discussion, Helen was told about the girl who insisted on seeing her. "Ask the young lady to come in," she said.

The girl entered the room, gripped the foot of the bed, and poured out her story. The man responsible for her condition had disappeared. She had no family, friends, or money. Then she clutched the actresses' hands and appealed for help. "Please help me," she pleaded. "I so want to keep my child!"

Helen called in her obstetrician. He examined the girl and discovered that the baby was due in less than a month. Charlie entered as the doctor was making out his report. "Everybody should be happy at a time like this," he said. He promptly made plans for the girl to stay with some of his friends. He also arranged for a doctor for the young woman and hospital care.

Dr. Virgil Damon, an assistant to Dr. Lobenstine, frequently went to the MacArthurs' home to check up on Helen's medical progress. "She and her husband were filled with sympathy and considerateness. They were loving and kindhearted parents but perhaps a bit too indulgent. There were very few things the child didn't have. She was only a few months old, and already her room was filled with blocks, books, rubber balls, dolls. I understand that they rarely came home without bringing her a gift. Once it was a five-foot stuffed teddy bear."

Although a nursemaid had been hired, her services were not needed much when Charlie and Helen were home. The two would sit in the child's room for hours. "Not because she's ours," Charlie would say, "but isn't she terrific?"

"Yes, she is," Helen would agree.

Harpo Marx, between New York appearances, frequently stopped by to see the infant. "She's a born comic," he said. "Already a lot funnier than Groucho."

Another visitor was Osgood Perkins, father of actor Anthony Perkins. He was particularly intrigued when the baby let out a series of piercing howls and regally pointed to the ceiling. The veteran performer, who had played the city editor in *The Front Page*, said, "That child's a faithful combination of her mother and father. Why, she just announced emphatically that if she's not cast as the lead cherub, she'll sock the producer in the eye!"

On the nurse's day off the MacArthurs delighted in wheeling Mary's custom-made English carriage. When passersby made flattering comments about the lovely infant, Charlie would bow. "Thanks," he would exclaim, puffing out his chest. "It was really easy to do—a labor of love." If the baby cried, he would proclaim to spectators, "You are privileged to hear the bawling of a future star!"

The MacArthurs had solemnly agreed that when Mary got older, she should be allowed to choose her own career. Yet, Charlie once told Donald Ogden Stewart, "My deepest wish is that she follow in her mother's footsteps. If Mary has inherited only one-tenth of Helen's talent, she'll wind up being a star. The only thing that worries me is bringing her up in the city. I wonder if it's good for her?"

Several weeks later, when the MacArthurs were crossing Eighty-sixth Street with the carriage, a speeding automobile almost ran them down. Charlie, who at the time was pushing the baby, hastily drew back to the sidewalk. Helen broke away and began running after the car, which had stopped behind a double-parked truck. Usually, a meek woman who does not say anything stronger than "pe-ew," she reached the auto, yanked the startled two-hundred-pound driver out of the door, slapped his face, and let out a stream of very strong language.

"I guess the peril to my child gave me a sudden shot of adrenalin," she told a neighbor afterward. "My Irish background must have been responsible for the rest."

The MacArthurs frequently walked to the La Petite Patisserie on York Avenue. Andrew Neuman, whose parents owned the bakeshop, often waited on them. "They'd bring their daughter's carriage right into the store," he recalled. "My mother would remark how pretty the baby was. Mr. MacArthur would say, 'Thank God, that she takes after her mother in that department.' Then he'd wait for his wife to add something to his statement. If she didn't speak right up, he'd remind her. 'You're supposed to say, Thank God she has her father's brains!' Then both of them would burst out laughing.

"When Mr. MacArthur came in alone, he'd buy dozens of croissants, brioche, pastry, cakes, and pies. Just about everything in the store. For the life of me, I never knew what he did with all that stuff. It was enough to feed an army."

When Mary was one year old, her parents decided to celebrate by giving her a gala birthday party. At the time sophisticated hosts tried to trot out distinguished celebrities to entertain their guests such as Ignace Paderewski, Irène Joliot-Curie, Arthur Conan Doyle, Haile Selassie. Charlie was determined that his daughter's birthday would be the top event of the year. He sent engraved Tiffany invitations that read: "Helen and Charles MacArthur request the honor of your august presence on the fifteenth of February to meet Scarface Al Capone. R.S.V.P."

Most of the guests recognized the jest. Lucrezia Bori, the operatic star, did not. She canceled a trip to Europe so that she could meet the notorious gangster. When Charlie told her that it was all a joke, she refused to believe him. All evening she kept insisting on confronting Capone. Finally, a desperate MacArthur made a long-distance call to a lawyer friend of his who represented the mobster. He explained his predicament. The lawyer agreed to help. Minutes later the prima donna was talking to the gangster, who was in Chicago:

"This is Lucrezia Bori, the opera singer."

"Yeah, an' I'm Little Bo Peep. You're some broad MacArthur's picked up."

"No. No. I'm truly who I say I am."

"Prove it!"

"All right. I'll sing for you." She held the receiver close to her bosom and sang the drinking song from *La Traviata*.

"Yeah, I know all about opera. You're really that canary you say you are. Thanks a lot for the personal song. Now, eat some ice cream and wish that kid a happy birthday for me."

Like many children, Mary had a baby book, but many of the inscriptions were unique. On that first birthday, Noel Coward had thoughtfully composed a message to Mary meant tenderly for her to read in her adulthood. He said that he hoped it would aid her in interpreting her unusual parents. It included, "Your mother is an actress, child. And consequently nuts. There's one more fact that you must list and face, for good and bad. Your father is a dramatist and necessarily mad."

F. Scott Fitzgerald also composed some verse for one of her later birthdays. He wrote that she possessed "portions of mama" and "dashes of a questionable pa." Another entry was by Alexander Woollcott. When

Mary came of school age, her parents decided to send her to a fashionable private academy in Englewood, N.J. They asked Woollcott to submit a letter of reference for his godchild. He agreed and immediately dispatched a note to the headmaster: "I implore you to accept this unfortunate child and remove her from her shocking environment."

Soon after penning the "certificate of character," the irascible drama critic had dinner with Bennett Cerf. He told the publisher, "A mere jest, that's what it was. Why, that child is undeniably a work of art. Clearly, the product of a loving mother and father."

7

"Heavy Cabbage" in Hollywood

Shortly after Mary's birth, Helen agreed to appear for two more weeks in *Coquette*—one week in Cleveland and the other in Rochester. "The Cleveland engagement," she said, "was necessary to be able to continue supporting my mother. I played Rochester so that I could afford to buy a painting by William Auerbach Levy."

Several months later, Helen portrayed an Irish harlot in a dramatization of Liam O'Flaherty's lusty novel *Mr. Gilhooley*. The first-night audience applauded politely but no more. It closed several weeks later. In the same season, she starred in an English import, *Petticoat Influence*. That play, a very light comedy, had better luck and ran on Broadway for four months. "But not long enough to please Charlie," said Ben Hecht, who had come in from Hollywood for a brief visit. "He didn't like it at all. 'With her talents', he told me, 'she may as well pull down some heavy cabbage out your way.' "

Many of MacArthur's friends from the Algonquin

Round Table group, including Benchley, Parker, Sherwood, Connelly, and Stewart, had gone to the West Coast to sell their talents. Charlie decided that he and Helen should do the same.

When he proposed leaving New York, Helen was frightened. She felt no ability to compete against what she called "the incredibly beautiful women" appearing on the silver screen. She was overcome by her old feeling of drabness. "I can't be a movie star," she said. "I'm just the plain girl next door."

At a party at Neysa McMein's, MacArthur picked Helen up in his arms and marched around the room singing, 'They ain't seen nothing 'til they've seen you, baby!" Reluctantly, she agreed to go.

One of the last things they did before boarding the Super Chief, the train that was to take them to California, was to divulge their support of their friend Heywood Broun, who was running for Congress on the Socialist ticket. After publicly announcing that they would vote for Broun, Charlie said, "Nobody in his right mind would want to be in Congress, but then Heywood always was a bit peculiar. All kidding aside, that body of lawmakers would be enriched by his august presence, be he a Socialist, God-fearing Holy Roller, or atheist Skip-Roper."

When the MacArthurs arrived on the West Coast, they found many invitations to dinners and parties already waiting. They felt they would need a fairly large and impressive house to reciprocate. After much hunting, they found a huge estate near the MGM studio in Culver City. The main dwelling, situated in the midst of twenty acres of artichokes and cruising turkeys, was so extraordinary that when Benchley visited it for the first time, he said, "I was so overwhelmed by their palatial residence that before taking my shoes off I wanted to run to the nearest tuxedo renting shop."

Charlie persuaded Irving Thalberg, the MGM production head, to cast Helen in *Lullaby*, later called *The Sin of Madelon Claudet*, a movie MacArthur had been asked to rewrite. It was not a very difficult request to grant as more than a dozen glamour queens had previously turned down the part of the Marseilles streetwalker.

Kay Francis, one of the actresses who had given Thalberg a flat rejection, told gossip columnist Louella Parsons, "I'd have to be out of my mind to play that silly French prostitute. Why, that dumb little bunny actually walked the streets so that she could make money to buy fancy clothes for her son. Phooey! How can any actress generate sympathy for such a shallow woman?"

Helen accepted the role with great enthusiasm. She had long wanted to appear in something Charlie had written. Before their marriage she had begged him to allow her to star in *Salvation*, the play he had collaborated on with Sidney Howard. "Sidney could have been easily persuaded," recalled Marc Connelly. "It was Charlie who was negative. He kept telling Helen that she just wasn't the proper type and that someday he'd write the correct vehicle for her. 'Until then,' he'd say, 'be patient!' "

Although she had been given the part of Madelon Claudet, the studio was still wary about her public image. "I wasn't something for the boys," Helen said. "I wasn't tall, long-legged, broad-shouldered or deep-bosomed like Joan Crawford. I didn't have Garbo's hollows under my cheekbones."

To try and make Helen more alluring, beauty experts and press agents proposed a large variety of remedies from false eyelashes to phony backgrounds. "She was having none of them," said Sadie Geller, who worked in the MGM publicity department. "My boss wanted to push the story about how Helen Hayes really was the love child of Broadway producer Charles Frohman and stage actress Maude Adams. When she refused to go along with it, he cooked up an even more fantastic biographical sketch. In this one she had been born an honest-to-God princess; her mother was an unwed showgirl; her father a playboy prince, who blew a hot trumpet in a three-piece combo; her grandfather the king. When she was a few days old her grieving mother was forced to give the infant up for adoption. . . . Pure unadulterated schmaltz. I don't blame Helen for saying no!"

Each night the film was in production, MacArthur carefully reworked his wife's next-day lines. When she was in front of the camera, he would hover nearby, making sure the director was giving her proper instructions. "Charlie became a watchdog on the set," Helen remembered. "The scenes he wrote for me were so wonderful and delicate. When Madelon got out of prison, she reached up and touched the branch of a tree—sensitive things like that. People thought I was a genius for having thought of that gesture. Well, it was all written down. Every body movement was indicated on his script. The marvelous writing was his gift to me."

MacArthur was working on another script when *Madelon Claudet* previewed. He was very tense and drinking heavily. Helen was too frightened to attend the screening and urged him to go alone. "Bennie, it was a terrifying experience," he later told Hecht. "The audience disapproved so violently that they actually stamped their feet and booed out loud. I offered to buy the picture so that I could burn it. Poor, poor Helen."

The following morning, while the MacArthur's were having breakfast, Charlie read the trade-paper reviews. They all agreed that the movie was awful. One said, "Miss Hayes should never have left Broadway."

"Tears rolled down my Charlie's cheeks," Helen recalled. "He thought that he had failed me, that because of his inadequate writing my screen career was doomed."

MacArthur fretted even more when Harry Rapf, a Metro executive, summoned Helen to his office. "You're a good actress," he said. "But you don't know your way in pictures. You just don't belong. We're going to shelve this one!"

Thalberg was out of the country when the film had been completed. As soon as he returned, he asked to see the movie. He was told, "That's a disaster we don't talk about." Thalberg insisted. After viewing it several times, he decided that several minor points were all that was wrong. Three days additional shooting was required. He then felt *The Sin of Madelon Claudet* was ready to be released.

This time when it previewed, neither Charlie nor his wife attended the screening. Instead, he and Helen visited friends who lived in Santa Barbara. Long after midnight an enterprising studio executive tracked the MacArthurs down. "Helen, I love you," he said excitedly. "The revised film is a pure gem. The audience ate it up and kept shouting for the star. I always knew you're a 110 percent genius!"

Helen reacted by jumping fully clothed into her host's swimming pool. A few seconds later Charlie followed. "I always knew my wife had 110 percent talent," he shouted gleefully. "And I was the one to bring it out!"

The Sin of Madelon Claudet, released in 1931, earned large profits for the studio. Helen won an Oscar for her portrayal of the French streetwalker. The film brought Helen worldwide acclaim. Charlie, however, received little credit. His name did not even appear on the screen credits. Reviewers ignored him. The trade papers that had snidely told Helen to return to Broadway now said, "Helen Hayes, we hope you'll stay in Hollywood forever."

In rapid order she appeared as Ronald Colman's co-star in Sinclair Lewis's *Arrowsmith*, played opposite Gary Cooper in the screen version of Ernest Hemingway's World War I novel *A Farewell to Arms*, and shared top billing with Clark Gable in *The White Sister*.

While she was making one of her early movies, Helen's dressing room was next to Marlene Dietrich's. On the first day of shooting, the glamorous German-born star approached Helen and in her husky, provocative voice said, "I hope you break a leg."

Helen was stunned. "I had heard that most Hollywood sirens were cats," she said. "But this was too much." That night at dinner she told Charlie about the incident. He laughed and explained that it was the European stage folk's way of wishing someone good luck. Show-biz people in America have since adopted the custom. But at the time it upset her considerably.

When Helen appeared opposite Gable in MGM's *The White Sister*, the "King of Hollywood" made a pass at her. She was so unnerved that she ran and hid in her dressing room. Only David Selznick himself was finally able to pry her out. "I'm sure Clark was only trying to be gallant," Selznick said. "Sometimes, even I wonder if she's some innocent babe in the woods or a wise old grandmother? Then I remember she's married to Charlie MacArthur. Anybody that has to play to him twenty-four hours a day has to be shrewd."

Ben Hecht recalled that once he visited Helen on the set. "It was the day before Christmas," he said. "There was a tradition at Metro that on December 24 all the MGM men ran out of their offices at noon and kissed the women who had the temerity to show up. The corridors became full of squeals and mating cries. I was escorting Helen to her dressing room when the pre-holiday whoop-de-do erupted. Suddenly, Louis Mayer spied Helen and seized her. Her response was something to behold. She sank her tooth into his neck!"

"As one film success followed another, Charlie seemed to feel that he was sort of a prince consort to a prominent actress," said Donald Ogden Stewart. "Her career was surpassing his. Inwardly, Charlie seemed to be changing. He didn't complain much. Maybe his drinking increased, if that were possible. But on the surface he was still the same 'good-time Charlie.' You could still count on him to do the unexpected."

Retired studio employees, like old newspaper reporters, also love to tell stories about Charles MacArthur. "He took the starch right out of stuffed shirts," said Ike Haigler, who had worked as a prop man for MGM and Paramount. "No one was safe with him around. Once, the big-shot producer Hunt Stromberg, a real Colonel

Blimp, walked high-nosed into Charlie's cubicle and bawled him out for not turning in a script on time. 'Weeks have gone by, and you're not even writing!' he yelled.

"Charlie put on a shocked expression. 'Your damn script is right here!' he angrily answered as he grabbed a large pile of letters from his desk. Then in front of Stromberg's eyes, he ripped them up into small bits. Before Stromberg could speak, Charlie shook his head miserably. 'Hunt, I have too much respect for your high standards to give you this junk. I want you to see only my best.'

"The producer apologized all over the place. He said he was sorry for his outburst and then swiftly left. That was when Charlie finally sat down at his typewriter and began the delayed scenario. He had it completed by the weekend."

MacArthur felt that the studio needed to learn humility. And that he was the man to teach it. He confided one of his plans to Marc Connelly. The service station Charlie frequented had just hired a good-looking English pump attendant named Joe Swaby. "He's never written more than a few misspelled postcards," MacArthur said. "But he has a lovely upper-class accent. The first thing I'll do is change his name to something fancy like Westminster Woollcott. Then I'll tell Bernie [Bernie Hyman, the production chief of Metro] that this brilliant English novelist and playwright is in L. A. for three days. I'll say, 'Westminster Woollcott is afraid that Hollywood will bastardize his art, and he refuses to work here. Bernie, that's where you come in. I'm convinced that only you can talk some sense into him.' "

"Bring him in," Bernie Hyman insisted after Charlie told him the story.

The next day Charlie pretended to drag the "brilliant English novelist" into Bernie's office. He had coached Swaby—now Westminster Woollcott—to say nothing and look disdainful. Hyman began his coaxing immediately. "This studio needs people like you. . . . Give us a try. . . . What can you lose? You'll never know unless you familiarize yourself with the goods. . . . I promise that we won't make you work on anything you feel beneath you. . . . How about a thousand dollars a week to start?"

At this point, Charlie, who was partly concealed behind a large India rubber plant, nodded to his protégé. The young man caught the signal and agreed to Hyman's terms. The happy production chief feverishly shook Westminster's hand. Then he threw his arms around Charlie and effusively thanked him. And to his new employee, he said, "Westy boy, you won't regret this!"

The former gas-station attendant worked at the studio for a year. He never wrote a thing, but each week he received his thousand dollars. When called upon to submit a scenario, he did what Charlie had told him: "Frown!"

"He became the best frowner in town," Connelly recalled. "Only someone like MacArthur could have dreamed up such a fantastic plot and made it work!"

Charles Lederer, another screenwriter, offered an additional anecdote: John Gilbert, the leading Hollywood matinee idol, had just ended a love affair with Greta Garbo. He was said to be heartbroken. Gilbert telephoned MacArthur and urged him to come posthaste to the hotel room where he was hiding. "If you're not here in exactly fifteen minutes I swear I'll kill myself!" he threatened. Gilbert who had often spoken of suicide added, "This time I mean it! Remember, in exactly fifteen minutes!"

Charlie broke all speed records getting to the hotel. He did not wait for the elevator but ran up the three flights of stairs. When he dashed into the actor's suite, he found the dejected suitor calmly eating an anchovy pizza and drinking a glass of milk.

"Keep feeding your damn pretty face," shouted an enraged MacArthur. "You've cried wolf for the last time!" He then snatched up Gilbert, who was still clutching the pizza, and carried him to an open window. "You may as well go on a full stomach!" he said as he stuffed a large slice into the terrified actor's mouth and dangled him out of the window.

MacArthur and Hecht were asked to write a screen adaptation of Emily Bronte's *Wuthering Heights*. As usual they procrastinated in production. When Alexander Woollcott, who regarded the book as one of his "favorite concoctions," heard about the delay, he decided to intervene. He upbraided the pair for their malingering and insisted they use his summer place in Vermont to do the writing. They accepted and flew east.

One weekend when Alec was in residence and harassing them beyond endurance, they composed a script especially for his eyes only. In it they had Heathcliff, the moody English hero, emigrate to Texas, where with two six-guns slung low on his waist, he tangled with cattle rustlers and Indians. He also got involved with a dance hall hostess who demanded that he marry her.

Charlie carefully left the script on top of his desk, where his host was sure to see it. As expected, Woollcott tiptoed into MacArthur's working room and peeked. He was dumbfounded. "You have raped Emily Bronte!" he shrieked.

"She's been waiting breathlessly for years," Charlie said cheerfully.

Another play writing triumph for the team of MacArthur and Hecht was *Twentieth Century*. As *The Front Page* had become the definitive newspaper epic, Hollywood and Broadway insiders called this one, "The best crazy comedy ever written about show business." Marc Connelly said, "It paved the way for all those that followed."

Twentieth Century premiered at Broadway's Broadhurst Theatre on December 29, 1932; ran for 154 performances; and was forced to close only because of the deepening Depression.

"The bankers were out to get me, one way or another," Charlie philosophized.

Although MacArthur made frequent trips to New York, he felt he was a "fat-cat prisoner in the land of heavy cabbage." Noel Coward observed, "I found that Charlie's facetious and eccentric behavior was often the chief topic of conversation at Hollywood parties. Celebrities would approach me and inquire about the tennis game I had with Charlie at two o'clock in the morning. I was asked to tell and retell that story. We used wire rackets which made the ball hop all over the court. It looked positively eerie in the moonlight. Immediately afterward Charlie plunged fully clothed into the swimming pool."

In Hollywood, MacArthur missed the fast and witty conversations of the Algonquin Round Table. His homesickness was assuaged slightly when Groucho Marx invited him to join the West Side Writing and Asthma Club. Members met for lunch once a week at Lyman's Restaurant, which was across the street from Hollywood's famous Brown Derby.

"Members of our hush-hush, private club," said Groucho, "are required to do two things: eat and complain!"

Membership in the secret organization was limited to fourteen. Groucho had voted himself president. "My social life revolved around these writers," the comedian said. "As the Algonquin wits gravitated west, they were taken up by our group. We had the elite and Charlie was the crème de la crème. I was in love with him, as was everyone else who knew him. He was without doubt the most charming guy I ever met."

At the first few luncheons that MacArthur attended he was very quiet. Then he introduced a secret handshake, which endeared him to Marx: Left hand under right knee; then grab your fellow member's hand firmly and wheeze three times.

"But that was peanuts compared to the other ideas he hatched at our table," recalled Groucho. "If I live to be 118, I'm sure I'll never see such brilliance again!"

Sadie Geller, the Metro publicist, agreed with Groucho. "Charlie would frequently come to our office and tell us how we could get lots more coverage for the studio. Each of his ideas was zanier than his last."

One of the suggestions was to put pictures of all the Metro performers on two-inch cards. Each one would be numbered on the top. Moviegoers would be given a free card every time they went to a theatre showing a Metro film. At the end of the year the winning numbers would be selected. The first prize would be movie contracts for the victor and his second cousins. The runner-up would get John Barrymore to act as his slave for one month with a year's option.

Another idea Charlie had to boost the studios who were having serious financial problems was to open their commissaries and charge the public for the privilege of sharing a meal with a Hollywood celebrity. "Naturally," said Sadie Geller, "his wife headed his list. Helen Hayes would bring $50. Clark Gable, Claudette Colbert, Fred Astaire, Irene Dunne, Ronald Colman, and others he particuarly liked brought $25 apiece. His list went all the way down to 2 cents for lunch with David Selznck."

For some unknown reason, Charlie hated Selznick. He could not look at him without getting into a fist fight. Once at a party at Harpo Marx's house Myron Selznick came over to Helen and said, "Do you think it's all right for your husband to be talking to my brother?"

"Oh, they seem to be getting on like a house on fire," she said.

Suddenly, Charlie and David were rolling on the floor. Selznick seemed to be getting the worst of it as MacArthur crushed him in a hammerlock. Irene Selznick, David's wife, took off her shoe and started beating

Charlie on the head with the three-inch spike heel.

Her repeated blows ended the brawl. Both men got up from the thick rug and flicked off imaginary dust. Then Charlie turned to the wide-eyed guests and bowed slightly. He said, "Now, I know why I like ladies in flat heels."

One Saturday night Mary's governess came down with the flu. Charlie and Helen had been invited to dinner at the home of Franchot Tone; Joan Crawford was Mrs. Tone at the time. After much discussion, the MacArthurs decided to keep the date and take Mary along. Helen dressed the child in a fetching pink dress and bonnet that her friend actress Ruth Gordon had bought in London. Sam Goldwyn, the legendary Hollywood panjandrum, was one of the guests. He was so taken with the child's beauty that he exclaimed to Frances, his wife, "That kid's a knockout. Already she's got a lot of class. If you promise to have one just like that I'll sit still for it." Then he turned to Charlie and added, "I want you to write a picture so I can star her in it. She's a natural."

Charlie thanked him. "Not just yet," he replied. "If ever."

Helen nodded in agreement.

The governess was still indisposed the following week. Once again the MacArthurs took their young daughter to a party. At this one, the hostess was Marion Davies. "We both were delighted with her company," Helen said. "And Charlie felt that her friend, William Randolph Hearst, was a good newspaperman."

In addition to bringing Mary, the MacArthurs

brought Marion a mammoth pot of artichokes that had been grown on their estate. "We have to give them away," Charlie explained. "As soon as they ripen, they attract millions of flies. Those damn flies are all over the house."

Later in the evening, with little Mary sound asleep in Marion Davies's huge four-poster, the adults played anagrams. They had to offer words and then rearrange the letters into another word. Charlie's contribution was *artichokes*. Stymied, the other guests quickly deferred to him. "Thackorites," he proudly exclaimed. When challenged, he had a ready reply: "Groups organized to administering blows to flies."

Donald Ogden Stewart also attended that party. He remembered that shortly after the anagram contest several of the guests did impromptu skits. "Everybody broke up," he said, "when MacArthur and Charlie Lederer, Marion's screwball nephew, recited a ditty they'd recently written about David and Irene Selznick. Irene was the ugly-duckling daughter of Louis B. Mayer, head of MGM. She had married David Selznick, who right after the ceremony became Mayer's heir apparent. The rhyme was hilarious:

> *Someone had to marry Irene Mayer.*
> *Someone had to have the guts to lay her.*
> *Someone had to woo her,*
> *Without tossing up his dinner.*
> *That's why our David was born.*

"I'm told that when Irene Mayer Selznick heard about the rhyme, she began to cry. Charlie learned of her misery. Instantly, he sent her several dozen long-stemmed roses. The enclosed card read: 'Apologies to a much misunderstood and beautiful lady. Charles Mac-Arthur.' In many ways, he was the last of a vanishing breed—a true gentleman."

8

Return to New York

The MacArthurs felt that they had stayed in Hollywood entirely too long. "I had ceased to be an actress," Helen said. "I had become a performer with a bag of tricks." More important, she had come to the conclusion that the tinsel-filled film capital was among the worst places in which to raise a child.

Her husband shared her views. "We started packing," he said, "a few seconds after Mary asked to be chauffeured around in style similar to that enjoyed by her best friend. This kid was ferried about in a twenty-seven-cylinder Dusenberg. It even had a built-in refrigerator that was loaded with caviar sandwiches and imported French lollipops. Helen and I wanted a normal, plain American upbringing for our daughter."

The "normal upbringing" seemed to mean a permanent move to their New York City apartment overlooking the East River. No sooner had they unpacked their trunks than Ned Sheldon insisted that Mary be baptized. "She's nearly six years old," he said firmly. "It's high time a minister sprinkled her with water. You want her to be a normal American, don't you?"

Reluctantly, the MacArthurs agreed to a religious service. It was held in Sheldon's living room. An altar was set up and decorated with a cross and white flowers. Charlie held out for a double set of godparents. "The kid is extraspecial," he said. "She deserves at least two of everything."

Sheldon's sister, Mary, and actress Ruth Gordon were appointed godmothers. Alexander Woollcott was selected as one of the godfathers. When he heard that there was to be a second one chosen, he objected vehemently. "The only doubles I permit," he fumed, "are the letters in my surname!" After much pleading, he sulkily allowed Sheldon, who was to be the other godfather, to join him in sponsoring the child.

At exactly four in the afternoon the baptismal ceremony began. Woollcott remarked, "It may be considered sacrilegious, but I do think the minister should heat the water before sprinkling it on her. If she catches cold, I'll never forgive him."

When the MacArthurs returned to their house on East End Avenue, the doorman, who was aware of the baptism, observed that Mary suddenly looked grown-up. "God will do that every time," said the six-year-old, who, it was plain, had inherited her father's talent for spontaneous bon mots.

Ben Hecht and Charlie decided to produce their own films in New York. "The movies they make in Hollywood are unreal," MacArthur lamented. "And besides, it's a crummy town to live in. Everybody out there is a genius, and to be anybody you've got to be a head genius. Well, you can't be a head genius until you go to a story conference with a doctor in attendance. Even with all the lettuce they give you, it isn't worth it."

The two mavericks rented a studio in Astoria, Long Island, where in 1934 for well under $200,000 they turned out *Crime Without Passion.* Claude Rains was cast as a corrupt lawyer who murders his mistress because he is tired of her. Although some critics called it a modern masterpiece, it did not make much money.

MacArthur and Hecht next produced *The Scoundrel,* starring Noel Coward. The sophisticated English playwright and composer made his acting debut in that movie. Charlie cast close friends in many of the minor roles. Alexander Woollcott played a gossipy fop. Robert Benchley was to have a cameo part as an alcoholic hog caller who suddenly loses his voice. At the last minute the role was eliminated. Benchley picketed the studio with a sign that read, "Hogs of the World, Unite!"

The next year *The Scoundrel* was also hailed by reviewers. It won MacArthur and Hecht an Oscar for their writing. But like *Crime Without Passion,* it was not a commercial success. The next MacArthur-Hecht creation made even less money. It was called *Once in a Blue Moon,* a spoof of the Russian Revolution, and this time the producers did not even achieve a critical success. A Boston reviewer called *Once in a Blue Moon* "the worst movie ever made."

He was kinder to their next film, *Soak the Rich:* "Ben Hecht and Charles MacArthur have moved up a notch. They are currently presenting the second-worst movie ever made. This clear-out film is about college radicals protesting the removal of a professor who advocates taxing only the very well-to-do . . . a ridiculous plot but many nimble-witted lines."

While Charlie was busy making films, Helen starred in a succession of prosperous Broadway hits: *The Good Fairy*, *Mary of Scotland*, and *Victoria Regina*. When she was cast as the six-foot-tall Mary Stuart in Maxwell Anderson's *Mary of Scotland*, she worried about appearing tall enough to play portray the statuesque queen. Mae West, who was her exact height, told her "Elevator shoes make me appear a mile high."

Helen had a pair made, but she was still shy nine inches. The deficiency did not seem to bother the audience. Dr. William Lyon Phelps, the distinguished professor of English at Yale University, came backstage after one performance. "Miss Hayes, you grow right in front of our eyes," he said. "You are every inch of Mary Stuart's six feet. How do you do it?"

Charlie, who was in her dressing room at the time, replied, "It's easy for my wife. She acts tall."

Her 969 performances in *Victoria Regina* were even more spectacular. From the start of the play to the final curtain, Queen Victoria ages more than fifty years. In the last two scenes, the sovereign's mouth and eyelids were supposed to droop and her cheeks to seem swollen. Helen could manage the first two but had trouble with the third. Charles Laughton suggested that she puff out her face by inserting half an apple in each cheek. It worked well enough through the first few minutes. But the apple tasted so good, she swallowed it. Thereafter, she inflated her cheeks with absorbent cotton.

She played the old queen so convincingly that one

man sitting in the fifth row nudged his companion and, pointing to the stage, demanded in tones clearly audible across the footlights, "Who is that woman? Nonsense, it can't possibly be Miss Hayes!"

Eleanor Roosevelt, who saw the play three times, said, "Never have I been so charmed by a stage characterization. I just couldn't stop clapping." Mrs. Henry Morganthau, Jr., wife of Franklin D. Roosevelt's secretary of Treasury, outdid her. She applauded steadily for twenty-two minutes.

Helen revealed how she impersonated Victoria so vividly. "As the basis for the old queen's character," she said, "I used my own grandmother, Graddy Hayes. I had a picture of her in my mind at every performance. I adopted Graddy's demeanor. Also, I could understand Victoria. She was a *Hausfrau* who happened to become an empress. I felt at home with her. And why not? I'm a *Hausfrau* who happened to become an actress."

Audiences were particularly quiet and reverent during the scene in which the feeble queen welcomes her family and subjects to her diamond jubilee. On New Year's Eve, theatregoers were abruptly jerked from the mood of reverence when Victoria pulled a red tin horn from the seat of her wheelchair and blew three loud blasts. Later a reporter asked Helen what prompted her to do it. "Charlie thought the audience needed to be jolted out of its reverie," she explained. "It sure did the trick."

The play about the dowager queen appeared on Broadway for 108 weeks. At the time, most of the bit players earned about $75 a week. Just before Christmas, *Victoria Regina* prepared to close its New York run. That is when Helen informed the bit players that since the play's opening she had been saving a dollar a week. "I thought you might like to have it as sort of a remembrance," she said. "You've all been so wonderful to me. Thanks and a Merry Christmas."

Actors glow when they discuss her. The affection is genuine. She is unquestionably one of the best-loved women in the American theatre. Vincent Price, who played Victoria's husband, Albert, said, "For three months I had the role in London, but this was to be my first Broadway appearance. I was cast opposite the great Helen Hayes. To put it mildly, I was extremely frightened. I soon learned that I needn't be. Despite her supreme ability and international reputation, I discovered that underneath she was a very humble person. At times she'd actually ask *me* how we played a scene in London. Working with her was pure joy. Over the years, we have become fast friends."

When *Victoria Regina* went on tour, it broke all existing records for the road. One night in a midwestern town it grossed $9,852. In one week, for six performances in the South, it took in $41,500. Its total earnings were $2,623,031. One of the cities it played in was New Orleans. The cast was booked at the luxurious Roosevelt Hotel. Helen decided that she would prefer to stay in the quaint French quarter. She selected a lovely old inn with wide columns and second-story porches. Charlie, who was in New York at the time, came to New Orleans several days later. He arrived at the theatre as his wife was being interviewed by several local reporters. He noticed that when Helen mentioned where she was staying the journalists' eyebrows rose and they looked incredulous. He soon found out why.

Eight-year-old Helen in her first Broadway role, Little Mimie in Victor Herbert's operetta, *Old Dutch*. A prophetic critic said, "I predict dainty Mistress Hayes will be with us for quite a spell." *Wide World*.

When Helen was 16—and looked about eleven—she applied for an ingenue role that required her to smoke a cigarette. The director found her coughing and spitting not very believable and urged her to stick to child parts. *Culver*.

Helen played opposite theatre great John Drew in *The Prodigal Husband*. Drew appreciated his own importance, but after the opening night performance remarked, "Tomorrow, she too, will be famous!" *Culver.*

Charlie at typewriter, while collaborator Ben Hecht stands close by. The two were so inseperable they were known as "Broadway's mischievous Siamese twins." *Academy of Motion Pictures.*

At age 31, sophisticated Charles MacArthur was heralded as a unique, daring writer of cynical comedy. *Culver*.

Helen—"who made Pollyanna seem like a painted hussy"—was 27 years old when she became Mrs. Charles MacArthur. *Wide World.*

Helen made a series of extremely profitable movies with leading Hollywood actors. *Above*:
Co-starred with Ronald Cole-
man in Sinclair Lewis' *Arrowsmith*. *Culver; Right*: Played opposite Gary Cooper in the screen
version of Ernest Hemingway's
World War I novel, *A Farewell to
Arms*. *Culver*.

From the start of *Victoria Regina* to the final curtain, Helen aged fifty years in her portrayal of the dowager queen. *Below:* Helen, a young Victoria, stands next to her stage husband, Albert, the Prince Consort, played by Vincent Price. *Culver; Right:* Helen Hayes as the old sovereign. *Culver.*

Left, Charlie adored his daughter. He'd often boast, "Why, the kid learned to walk by hanging onto the sides of a billiard table I bought her." *Culver*; *Below*: Actress Tallulah Bankhead once said, "What sheer inspiration joining Helen and Charlie together. When God made that match, He was even wiser than I am." *Culver*.

Above: Charlie and Helen at a masquerade party given by perennial hostess Elsa Maxwell. MacArthur's French sailor outfit won first prize. *Wide World; Right*: The relationship between Helen and Mary was extremely close. The youngster said, "I want to grow up exactly like my mother." *Culver*.

Above: Mary MacArthur and her brother Jamie play a piano duet as their beaming mother looks on. *UPI*. *Below*: Helen's mother, Catherine Hayes Brown, counsels her daughter and granddaughter. *Culver*.

Left: Helen and her 16-year-old daughter take joint bows after a hugely successful opening night performance of *Alice-Sit-By-the-Fire*. UPI. *Below*: It was a glorious moment for Helen and Charlie as they watched their 17-year-old son, James MacArthur, make his television debut. *UPI*.

Helen looks on proudly as Broadway's Fulton Theatre is renamed in her honor. *Wide World*.

Above: The MacArthurs toast each other at a ball given to commemorate Helen's fifty years on the stage. One thousand guests attended. *Wide World*. *Right*: After Charlie's death, friends felt Helen's only salvation lay in acting. Reluctantly, she appeared in *Anastasia*. *Culver*.

Left: Helen and her 19-year-old son have a little difficulty in getting adjusted to their hairstyles. James in a Delaware Indian coiffure for a Disney film. His mother's hair bleached snow-white for a stage role. *UPI.* *Below*: Helen, son Jim, and his two children, Mary and Charles. *Wide World.*

Helen in front of "Pretty Penny," her twenty-room Victorian house in
Nyack, N.Y.

Two longtime friends, Helen and Lillian Gish, relax in a horsedrawn carriage during an outing in New York's Central Park. *UPI*.

The lovely old inn she had chosen was the city's leading bordello.

When Helen played Queen Victoria in Washington,
D. C., Mrs. Roosevelt invited her to dine at the White
House. The actress discovered that the dinner party was
a very small one. It included the president, his wife,
their daughter Anne, Secretary of State Cordell Hull,
and Mrs. Hull. The president entered the room and
greeted Helen with "And how is Your Majesty?"

During the soup course, Mrs. Roosevelt reminded
her husband that shortly after dinner there would be a
large reception. "The president groaned," Helen recalled. "He said he was in no mood to shake hands.
Then Mrs. Roosevelt asked me if I would stay behind
and chat with him in the study."

When the two were alone FDR talked about the State
of the Union message that he was to deliver in a few
days. He wanted to know what she thought he should
say.

"*You* are asking *me*?" she asked unbelievingly.

"Miss Hayes," he replied, "you have no ax to grind.
I'd like to have your thoughts."

"For the next thirty minutes," Helen said, "the President of the United States listened to a suddenly
tongue-tied actress try to offer ideas."

She had further encounters with presidents. When
Dwight D. Eisenhower was in the White House, Mamie
invited Helen for a swim. It was a hot day. Helen was
appearing in Washington in *Mrs. McThing* and asked if
she might bring the children in the cast along with her.
Mamie graciously said, "By all means."

Leaving the young actors splashing under the watchful eyes of a Secret Service man, Mamie and Helen went to the upstairs family room. Suddenly, the president appeared at the poolside. "Who are those children?" he wanted to know. When they saw him, one shouted, "Cheese it, it's Eisenhower!" and off they all ran.

A few years later Helen was asked by President John F. Kennedy to make a twenty-six-nation goodwill tour for the State Department's cultural-exchange program. "I felt completely at ease with him." Helen said. "He was the kind of Irishman I had known all my life."

After the final performance of *Victoria Regina*, Helen, accompanied by her husband, journeyed to Chicago to fight a $100,000 alienation-of-affection suit brought by Carol Frink. Charlie's first wife contended that Helen Hayes had "maliciously and willfully" stolen MacArthur's love.

In a tearful voice Carol said, "I knew from the start that he was different." She quoted Charlie as saying immediately after their wedding ceremony, "I'll probably be hard to domesticate, for I'm a genius."

Carol declared, "I was more than willing to stand his eccentricities." She said he made love by stepping on her toes and that he insisted on moving from furnished apartment to furnished apartment because all the beds in Chicago were too short. Once, she testified, she and MacArthur rode to the West Coast in a single berth from which he went out to the dining car at mealtime and got something to eat. "He only brought me back an orange," she said. "That went on for the entire trip."

She also testified that "several times he told me it made him nervous to have me around while he worked. So I'd get out and walk the streets and call him up from time to time until he told me I could come home. . . . We parted temporarily because of money troubles. But we didn't mean it. We were still in love. Then along came Miss Hayes and snatched him away."

Against her complaint, depositions were offered by Robert Benchley, Marc Connelly, Ben Hecht, and Alexander Woollcott. They stated that Helen did not meet MacArthur until after the separation. Trembling, the actress said that because of her special request the suit was forced to trial. "I wanted the whole story brought into the open," she whispered. "It has caused a great deal of adverse publicity for years. I wanted to be cleared before the public, which supported me and trusted me. I wanted to be cleared, too, because I have a child growing up. I didn't want to feel that my husband would be considered culpable in any way."

Charlie was called briefly to the stand to identify some letters alleged to have been written by him to Carol. He quickly charmed the spectators, who were admonished by the judge to cease applauding. When one lady continued, the sergeant-at-arms stepped forward to eject her. She was allowed to remain when she explained she was hard of hearing and had missed the judge's warning.

"In that case," said Charlie, "I'll speak up." He answered all the questions in a loud, clear voice:

Q: Is that your handwriting?
A: I don't know, it's pretty sloppy writing. That's twenty years ago, and I've changed since.
Q: Well, read the contents, and say whether you wrote it.

A: I guess so; I wrote things like that twenty years ago.

Q: It's signed, "The Big Slob." Is it you?

A: In 1920 I called myself the Big Slob. Don't you think I'm a lot neater now?

Q: We're not here because of your neatness. Stick to the matter at hand. Here's a letter that's signed, "Charliekums." Is that your signature?

A: I'll always make a reservation about that name. It was given to me. It wasn't one I chose.

Q: But is it your handwriting?

A: I don't think so. Not the "kums." I think the "kums" has been added.

For three days newspapers across the country printed headlines about the celebrated case. Reporters clamored for firsthand information. Nothing was sacred. One gossip columnist asked Charlie if he wore pajamas when he was married to Carol. MacArthur had to be restrained from hitting him. When Charlie regained his composure, he snapped, "Instead of asking damn fool questions like that you should inquire if I'm glad I was married before?"

Then in Socratic fashion he answered his own query. "Yes," he replied. "I'm damn glad! In that way I can compare how wonderful a wife Helen is!"

On the third day of the trial, Carol suddenly called off the suit and paid court charges. Through her attorney she said she was sorry for the nasty remarks she had made about MacArthur and that there had been no malice whatsoever on the part of Helen Hayes when she became engaged to Charlie.

Triumphantly, the MacArthurs returned to New

York where they found a great pile of congratulatory telegrams from their friends as well as from Helen's fans. Among the senders were F. Scott Fitzgerald, Eleanor Roosevelt, Norma Shearer, Thornton Wilder, Sinclair Lewis, Tallulah Bankhead, and Maxwell Anderson.

Charlie greatly enjoyed the apartment and spent hours when he should have been writing looking through the windows at the action on the always interesting East River. He saw visitors constantly boarding the ferry to Welfare Island, which housed a large mental hospital. One sunny afternoon he urged Helen to accompany him there. Bea Lillie, who had just bought an apartment in their building, asked if she might come along.

"It was a beautiful day," Helen recalled. "We decided to make a grand tour of the island." After several hours of prowling around, the three realized it was time to get back, since Bea and Helen had performances that night. They returned to the ferry house. A suspicious-looking guard asked them for their visitors' passes. They had failed to get any. The guard made it clear that he thought they were patients trying to escape. To make matters worse, Helen told him, "I'm Helen Hayes, the actress, and this is Bea Lillie, Lady Peel! And this is Charles MacArthur, the famous playwright!"

"Yeah," the guard replied. "And I'm Napoleon Bonaparte!"

Outraged, Charlie advanced with clenched fists. Other uniformed men appeared quickly and marched the sputtering trio to a nearby police room. Again, Helen tried to tell a disbelieving sergeant who they were. He, too, dismissed her impatiently. "Lady," he said, "you're allowed one phone call. Then I'm calling the wagon."

She wondered who they should get. Bea suddenly remembered that her doctor, Morton Rodgers, the brother of composer Richard Rodgers, was in charge of a clinic on the island. She called him. His secretary said that he had left for the day.

"We'll be here for hours," Helen lamented.

"That's the end of tonight's performance," Bea agreed.

"What they need are some black eyes," Charlie muttered. He was clearly enjoying himself. Always the Chicago reporter, he happily anticipated the news stories when the facts got out.

Fortunately Dr. Rodgers, who had forgotten some papers, telephoned his Welfare Island office. His secretary told him about Bea's call, and he rushed to the rescue. Helen and Bea managed to get to their theatres minutes before curtain time. But that night their empty stomachs growled as they recited their first-act lines. Charlie went to Tony's, where he refused all solid food in deference to the starving ladies.

Although the MacArthurs loved the city, they often worried about whether it was a good place to raise their daughter. One afternoon, on the nurse's day off, a very tired Helen and a hungover Charlie took Mary to the Central Park Zoo. Walking along the grimy city streets, Helen decided that the child needed a backyard and an attic. Charlie said the youngster should have a dock to anchor the sailboat he planned on getting her.

Shortly afterward, one of their neighbor's children was kidnapped. The two-year-old son of a well-known lawyer who lived several floors below them was snatched from his stroller while his English nanny was in a store buying a magazine. Although the police found the youngster the following day, Helen and Charlie were badly shaken by the incident. They were convinced that they must move from the city and find a place in a more secluded area.

After much searching, they discovered an early Victorian house in Nyack, New York, where MacArthur had spent his childhood. "I loved the place from the moment I saw it," Helen said. "It was covered with gingerbread trim and had an enclosed widow's walk perched on the roof. On a clear day you could see for miles up and down the Hudson River. There were beautiful trees and lawns that sloped down to the water. I knew the MacArthurs had finally come home."

9

"To Nyack, to Nyack We Go"

"Charlie called me up in the middle of the night," said Ben Hecht. " 'Get your carcass out here by return mail!' he ordered. Then he sang some silly ditty: 'To Nyack, to Nyack we go, / Plenty of fun, earning big dough.'

"Rose and I moved to a house on a modest side alley, about a football field away. We rarely regretted it. True, he was the kind of neighbor who borrows your lawn mower and returns a coffeepot."

Nyack is a small town; the population is still sixty-five hundred. It was founded by the Dutch three hundred years ago. The site is one of the first breaks in the western palisades of the Hudson Valley where one can come ashore without climbing a cliff. Superb old trees and flowering shrubs grace hundreds of Victorian houses, large and small. They have stained-glass windows, Gothic decoration, round towers, and scalloped shingles. "Although only thirty miles from Times Square," Charlie once said, "Nyack rides on the river all alone. If one day the whole of Manhattan Island floated out to sea, people out here would never know or care."

Charlie had invoked the help of everyone he knew in finding a house but in the end the MacArthurs had come across it by accident—they drove by just as a "for sale" sign was being posted.

Shortly after they moved in, Helen had to go on tour with a play she was appearing in. Charlie decided to surprise her. He made a trip to Greco's paint store and asked for color samples. "The wife's away," he said. "Thought it would be nice to paint the house."

"A wonderful idea," replied Mr. Greco. "I'm sure she'll be pleased when she gets back. White, yes?"

MacArthur put his elbows on the counter and surveyed the paint pots. "How about a bright raspberry pink?" he said. "With a shiny maroon trim?"

The paint dealer's elbows joined him on the counter. "Mr. MacArthur," he said, "why don't you wait for the lady to come home before you decide?"

The house stayed white.

Helen Hayes was accustomed to being the center of attention. When customers at the local five-and-ten-cents store stared at her, she said to Mary, who had accompanied her there, "I'll wager that they will soon ask for my autograph."

Sure enough, a woman wearing a torn baseball cap and a pair of faded blue sneakers tapped her on the back. "Dearie," she whispered. "Your slip is showing a whole lot. Better fix it before others join the free show."

Indeed, one of Helen's shoulder straps had broken and her lacey undergarment was dipping toward the floor. The townspeople may have been aware of her stage triumphs, but to them she always was just plain Mrs. Charlie MacArthur, housewife.

She realized she belonged when she had to wait her turn at the grocery store. There were three women ahead of her. "Ladies, you can eat some of these pickles while you wait," the clerk said. "Compliments of the house."

Helen, who loved all vinegar products, reached into the pickle barrel and removed a handful. "Mrs. MacArthur, please!" he muttered sharply. "Only one to a customer! They are big pickles!"

Charlie was amused when his wife told him about the incident. Unlike Helen, he loved to have shopkeepers covet his patronage. And he charmed them all with his dialogues. Typical were the lines he and the owner of the local stationery store invariably exchanged:

Storekeeper: A very good afternoon to you.

Charlie: What's good about it? My dog just deposited a load on the living-room rug, the kitchen ceiling sprung a leak, and my car hit a tree stump on the way here.

Storekeeper: Well, that's life. What will it be today?

Charlie: I want a copy of the *Wabash Cannonball Gazette.*

Storekeeper: Sorry we don't have it.

Charlie: Then a copy of the *Sheepherder and Beekeeper Bugle.*

Storekeeper: I'm sorry we don't have that either.

Charlie: And you call yourself a stationery store! I'll settle for the *Rockland Journal News!*

Storekeeper: I thought you had it delivered.
Charlie: Yeah, but the dog dumped a load on that, too!

MacArthur conducted another long running ceremonial with the town druggist:

Druggist: How are things going?
Charlie: For one thing they're putting more brown paper in the Bull Durham all the time.
Druggist: I'm afraid that's a sign of our times. What can I get for you?
Charlie: I'd like 5 cents of your best liniment.
Druggist: Got a sore back?
Charlie: Not my back. It's for a cantankerous mule.
Druggist: Didn't know you had a mule.
Charlie: Got one all right. Know what he says? "There's no mule like an old fool!"

The druggist recalled that despite it being an absurd joke, he always laughed uproariously. He and the other shopkeepers agreed that Charlie was "truly a card."

Sometimes Mary accompanied her father on his rounds. She loved to say, "Oh, Pop, you're being silly again."

Charlie would feign displeasure. "That's the kind of respect I get from my own flesh and blood," he would reply. But it was obvious that he was delighted with her response. The two of them would leave the store holding hands.

"Poor Charlie," mused Helen. " 'All these years,' he'd say, 'I thought I was clever and funny. And then along comes Mary and my ego flies out of the window.'

He adored that child. Woe to anyone who upset her."

Once Billy Rose, the pint-sized Broadway showman, was asked for his definition of a best friend. He said, "A guy you can call in the middle of the night and he'll drop everything and come over without asking questions. Someone like Charlie MacArthur. He's one of my best friends."

Charlie was told about Rose's remarks. A bewildered look appeared on his face. "Helen," he asked. "what did I ever do to Billy Rose that he should call me his best friend?" Then he added, "Billy doesn't have a best friend!"

MacArthur later explained the reason for his ill-humor: an incident that occurred during the run of *Jumbo*. He said, still angry, "Ben and I wrote *Jumbo*. Rose produced it. He threw a party for the members of the cast. I took Mary. She was about nine years old at the time. Rose spotted her and asked if she'd like to own one of the ponies in the show. I saw the kid's eyes shine with joy. But I knew from previous experience with Billy that he had no intention of giving away one of the ponies.

"He had always been a four-flusher. I didn't want to disillusion Mary right then. But then I thought about it and told her that all her life she would meet men like Rose who would promise her things just to see her eyes light up. Men who had no intention of keeping their promises. . . . I was so right, the SOB never did give her that pony!"

"At the time Nyack had a few other colorful characters," said Hecht, "athough none of them possessed Charlie's tang or sweetness. There was Oom the Omnipotent, a former barber who started up a Yoga school and kept a full grown elephant and peacocks to guard it. Also there was an old lady who patrolled the village streets wearing a white robe and a jeweled crown. At each crossing, she'd lustily blow on a gold trumpet. A favorite of Charlie's was a mild-mannered woman who was a devoted animal lover. She didn't trust automobiles and would drive around town in a horse-drawn buggy. On cold winter days, she'd dress the horse in two pairs of pants made of imported Harris tweed."

At first, the furnishings in the Nyack house consisted largely of orange crates. Gradually, the MacArthurs decorated it with choice Victorian fittings. A museum curator who specialized in the nineteenth century was so impressed that she said, "They have some of the finest pieces found in any private house. I can see why they named the place Pretty Penny. Even then it must have cost a mint."

Notable were gilt-edged mirrors that reflected crystal chandeliers. On a small marble-topped table in the living room there was a plaster cast of Helen's hands holding an old-fashioned nosegay of fresh flowers. The master bedroom, which also served as a library, contained an almost life-sized sculpture of a Persian warrior's horse. Alfred Lunt had given it to Alexander Woollcott, who, he said, loaned it to MacArthur.

Charlie had designed the room around the horse and refused to return it. Periodically, Woollcott threatened to bring him into court if he failed to give it back. Mac-Arthur's response was to hang a picture of Alec in the adjoining bathroom just above the toilet. The lid was a gilt and velvet throne on which sat the stuffed shape of a willowy damsel in a tight-fitting corset and lace pantaloons.

The basement was all Charlie's. The two chief attractions were a king-sized bar and a shooting gallery. Guests had to be careful not to aim at the liquor bottles. MacArthur wanted to use photographs of Broadway critics as targets, but Helen objected. "They have always been kind to me," she said.

"Why not?" Charlie replied. "Saying anying derogatory about Helen Hayes is like spitting on the flag! And what's more, if they get tough they know they have to deal with me!"

John Barrymore, who was a houseguest at the time, joined in the conversation. "The splendiferous and magnificent Helen Hayes is so American," he said, "that Betsy Ross is about to be reincarnated in order to embroider Helen's likeness on the flag."

"The Great Profile," as Barrymore was often called, had telephoned MacArthur from Ben Hecht's house to say he was out of cigarettes. "May I stop by to borrow a pack?" He stayed for three days. His greatest pleasure was to lie in front of the living-room fireplace and read aloud from *Leaves of Grass*.

Several years before that, Gene Fowler and Charlie launched the "John Barrymore Rescue Mission." Their sole aim was to save the actor from drink. "This was a difficult thing to do," said Marc Connelly, "since Gene, who appointed himself president, and Charlie, master-of-arms, were well-known boozers themselves. But they sure tried. They'd invent unique cures. Once they took Barrymore, who was really loaded, to a remote area in southern Arizona. He was supposed to dry out there. They deposited him in a rundown church and left him in care of a teetotaling, water-drinking reverend who was a leading member of the Anti-Saloon League."

The following Saturday they visited the church and found Barrymore and the clergyman both thundering drunk. When the minister was sober enough to be understood, he said, "Mr. Barrymore convinced me that a true Christian gentleman loved his brother. And since my brother needed a drink badly I gave him my bottle of Dr. Hooplemeister's Restorative Elixir that I was keeping for a sore back or when I came down with an attack of pleurisy. We soon finished the bottle, and I borrowed lots more from my flock."

"Such ingenuity calls for a drink," said Charlie. "Where can we appropriate some more bottles?"

Barrymore always managed to escape. He then would call Charlie from some remote area and beg for his help. Once the plea came from Cinca, California, a tiny town near the Nevada border. Barrymore could not remember how he had gotten there. MacArthur, as usual, came to the rescue. The actor met Charlie's car as it pulled up to the village's only boardinghouse. He was surrounded by a howling mob of autograph seekers. When they saw him run up to MacArthur and embrace him, they wanted to know who the stranger was. Barrymore pretended shock at their ignorance. "Shame!" he bellowed. "Do you not recognize the Bastard King Charles of France? I command you to kneel!"

MacArthur interrupted the actor. "Please, no kneeling," he said. "I've grown democratic in your country. Just salute me!"

Many of Charlie's friends were equally bizarre. Leaving Mary with her governess, the MacArthurs set out for England aboard the S.S. *Manhattan*. The first night out they met an old acquaintance, Major William Beaufort, a British peer who loved to talk about his political and military experiences in "Inja." Charlie invited him to share cocktails in the lounge. Beaufort accepted and arrived a few minutes late. He was stark naked except for a pair of argyle socks and white suede shoes. "So sorry about being tardy, old sport," he said casually. "Couldn't find the proper tie."

A steward summoned several able-bodied seamen, who quickly carried the nude major off to the ship's hospital. Charlie apologized for his friend's attire. "His malaria keeps coming back," MacArthur explained. "When it does, Beaufort sweats a great deal and has to remove some clothing."

Two days later Charlie was involved in an even greater scandal. He and fellow passenger Eleanor Holm, champion backstroke swimmer and leading member of the Olympic team, engaged in a mammoth drinking session. Avery Brundage, president of the International Olympic Committee, who was also on the ship, promptly dismissed her for "participating in a deplorable alcoholic debacle with a member of the opposite sex."

The following morning MacArthur woke up with a colossal hangover. When he saw his wife furiously stuffing her clothing into suitcases, he asked, "Why are you packing? We don't get to Southampton for several days."

"I'm not going there," she snapped. "When the boat stops in Ireland, I'm getting off. I can't stand to be on the same boat with you and your friend Miss Holm. Mr. Brundage just tossed her off the team because of your shameful performance!"

"If I didn't have a splitting headache," Charlie said, "I would punch Brundage right in the nose. Doing such a thing to a fine woman like Eleanor Holm!"

"Fine woman, indeed," Helen sobbed. "Then what does it make the rest of us ladies—a pack of stick-in-the-muds?"

"Oh, you are not like that," Charlie said as he gave his wife a most angelic smile. Helen did not get off in Ireland.

In Nyack, the MacArthurs rarely accepted social invitations. Helen would have a maid tell callers that the mistress was sick in bed with a terrible headache. Charlie also had a surefire excuse to turn down invitations. In a thick, slurring voice he would simply explain that he was much too drunk to go anywhere. "It always worked," MacArthur said. "There are two things most people are sympathetic about: booze and headaches."

For hours he and his wife would sit in front of the marble fireplace in the living room. Helen would knit sweaters and wool hats for Mary while Charlie played mournful Scottish airs on the clarinet he had won when he wagered that *Salvation*, the play he had collaborated on with Sidney Howard, would be a failure. "I won the bet," he said, "when it closed down the following night."

Occasionally, this passion for privacy caused some bewilderment. Mel Harrow, a retired newspaperman, lived near the MacArthurs. He wanted to talk shop with Charlie and asked him over to his house. "He always refused," Harrow said. "He'd tell me that he'd been hitting the juice something fierce and was in no shape to go visiting. I was worried about him because I had been a heavy drinker myself and knew what effect it had on my work. I sent him a batch of material on how to stop emptying the bottle and I still remember the letter he sent in reply: 'The good Lord put alcohol on this earth to serve His good purpose. I don't know what that purpose is but I aim to find out.' "

Alan Hall, another would-be visitor, was an editor of *Time* magazine's "People" section. He planned to run an item about Helen Hayes and talked to her on the telephone. When he mentioned that he and his wife lived in Nyack and had long admired the MacArthurs' house, Helen invited them over for a drink. The following evening when they arrived, a servant showed them downstairs to the bar and said that Miss Hayes was on a long-distance call. They sat there for two hours when she sent word that she was sorry but had to go to bed with a sick headache.

Away from Nyack Charlie and Helen continued to maintain their active social life. Shortly after the Hall incident, they attended an elaborate party at the Waldorf Astoria hosted by producer Gilbert Miller. At midnight Helen said to Miller, "Charlie is having too much fun to leave now. I've got an early rehearsal and want to slip away. He's a bit high. I'd appreciate your seeing to it that he gets to bed safely."

Miller assured her that he would personally attend to it. When the festivities ceased, he faithfully bundled MacArthur into his car and drove to Nyack. When he got there an hour later, he found the house shut tight. He honked his horn and shouted. No one appeared.

After a careful search, he concluded that the house was empty. He turned around and drove back to New York City. Charlie spent the night on a couch in Miller's apartment.

Early the next morning a very agitated Helen phoned the producer. "What have you done with my husband?" she asked.

"He's sleeping it off in my house," Miller told her. Then he said that he had driven to Nyack and found the house deserted. "So I had to return to the city."

"Good heavens," said a mortified Helen. "I forgot to tell you that we moved into the Waldorf for the winter."

Helen was well-known for her absentmindedness, but the feature that really set her apart from other actresses was her very casual and unassuming wardrobe. "All the other stars would leave the theatre wearing fur coats, fancy hats, and imported French shoes," said Pop Stern, a longtime stage-doorman. "Not Miss Hayes. She'd always wear a simple kind of a dress and a plain wool coat."

One drama critic wrote, "Helen Hayes is the worst dressed actress on the American stage."

A syndicated columnist disagreed with his evaluation. "It isn't that she dresses badly," she said. "Helen Hayes simply doesn't dress at all."

Charlie was upset by all the talk about his wife's unfashionable clothes and determined to turn her into a stylish lady. He phoned Revillon Frères, an exclusive fur shop, and inquired about a sable coat. A clerk told him they had an elegant one at $15,000.

"Fine," he said. "I'll send my wife around to pick it up."

The next day Helen had a matinee performance. After leaving the theatre she walked to the fur store. On the way, she passed the Durand-Ruel Galleries and saw a Renoir painting in the window. "It was labeled *Girl in a Lace Hat*," she recalled. "To me, it was a portrait of Mary—how she would look in a few years. I went in and priced it. It was $15,000, the exact price of the sable coat. I bought the painting."

"My wife may not be the world's best financier when it comes to handling money," Charlie once told Marc Connelly, "but she knows exactly how she wants to spend it. When she was growing up, money came hard. She's never forgotten that period.

"Come to think of it, buying that Renoir painting was a pretty shrewd investment. In a few years, I bet it will double in value. I'm also that way. When it comes to walking or taking a taxi, I always choose the taxi. That way I save on shoe leather. Pretty damn smart!

"But despite all that," MacArthur added, "some people think we're spendthrifts. There's a rumor we even have our initials engraved on the water faucets— H and C."

10
Enter Jamie

W anted lots of children," Helen said. "Ten of them. A numerologist once told me that ten is my lucky number: I was born in Washington, which has ten letters; my name also has ten letters; I arrived in this world on the tenth day of the tenth month. But only Mary appeared on the scene. Charlie and I consulted several specialists. We were told that there was nothing wrong with either of us. Still—no baby."

She began to suffer from severe migraine headaches. This went on for several years. One doctor suggested that grief or frustration might be the cause. "Anything troubling you?" he asked.

"Yes," the actress replied. "I can't seem to have another child."

"That might well be responsible for your headaches," he told her. "Have you thought about adoption? If you did, the migraines might disappear."

Helen felt that her husband would not like the idea.

"But I was wrong," she said. "As ever. Charlie took the large view. We put in our application."

The result was a baby boy. MacArthur was the first member of the family to see his new son. He said humbly that the child did the adopting. "He gave me the once-over carefully," Charlie said. "I must have passed muster because he nodded and grinned as if to say, 'It's okay. I'll join your clan!' "

After the baby arrived in Nyack, Charlie tiptoed upstairs to Mary's room and placed him on her bed. He then called in his daughter and said, "Here's a present for you. A little brother."

Mary, who was about to celebrate her ninth birthday, was thrilled. She turned to Helen, who was standing beside her. "Mummy," Mary asked. "Did he come out of you?"

Her mother explained that he had not. That God had given the child to them. The three MacArthurs looked down at tiny James Gordon MacArthur. "Now we're a real family," Charlie said.

The following day he made his usual rounds of Nyack shops. Only this time his opening gambit was changed:

Storekeeper: A very good morning to you.

Charlie: Yes, it's a very good morning.

Storekeeper: (surprised) Did I hear right? Did you say that it was 'a good morning'?

Charlie: That's surely what it is. The MacArthurs have a brand new kid. He's extra-special. Fills his diaper with golden nuggets.

Storekeeper: Congratulations. What will it be today?

Charlie: Some Bull Durham for the kid.

Storekeeper: (disbelieving) You're giving chewing to-
bacco to an infant?
Charlie: You heard right. Lots better than having him
chewing up the expensive antiques!

Old-timers fondly remember MacArthur wheeling
Jamie's carriage and buckling Mary's roller skates. "He
was a darn good father," said octogenarian Edna Ward,
"even if he was kind of an oddball. Like the time he
made them a snowman and dyed it bright purple. Then
what does he do? Puts on chin whiskers and tops it off
with an Indian headdress full of different-colored
feathers. He sent a picture of it to the local paper."
Her sister, Agnes, had also lived in Nyack. "I heard
MacArthur was a mighty fine photographer," she added. "Had all sorts of fancy cameras. They say he used to
follow his wife around and snap her in the altogether.
A favorite joke was to tease her by slipping strange lin-
gerie under his pillow and pretending it belonged to a
mysterious female caller. But Helen was never annoyed
because she was never fooled, not even the first time.
Everybody in town knew how much he delighted in
his wife."
"Charlie was the kindest of fathers," Helen said. "He
was more than just a male parent. He was their play-
mate."
One night at dinner, Charlie told Mary that it was
high time she learned how to shoot mashed potatoes.
He explained, "The skill comes in very handy when a
person at the table becomes too stuffy. This is how you
put a stop to it. You take a big helping of mashed potatoes on your spoon. Now you turn the spoon around
like this. Then you take your right thumb and place it

on the top of the spoon. Wth a flick of your wrist you send it off."

MacArthur's mashed potatoes hit Miss Astrid, Mary's Norwegian governess, right in the middle of her forehead. Helen did not believe that Charlie had planned it exactly that way, but he was pleased when it happened. He said he thought Miss Astrid was getting too pompous.

Helen called upon her husband to administer corporal punishment to the children when it was needed. But Charlie rarely spanked. "There are better ways," he said, never explaining what they were. The two exceptions both involved Jamie—once when the five-year-old boy tried to crawl out of a window onto the roof and ten years later when he came home at 2 A.M.

The MacArthurs believed that children should be reared in the company of dogs. "Our house was always a kennel," Helen said. "The patter of our youngsters' feet was often drowned by the patter of paws."

Sambo was the first dog they owned. He was a poodle; MacArthur identified himself as a "poodle man." Sambo loved to eat felt hats, especially gray ones. Another of his pleasures was to receive flattery. He would snap at Charlie's heels until MacArthur crooned to him that he was the most beautiful animal in the world.

The next poodle was imported from England. He was named Turvy—short for *topsy-turvy*—because in a very few seconds he would turn the household upside down. Devoted to Helen, the dog was jealous of Charlie. As soon as MacArthur put his arms around Helen, the dog would begin to howl. A more intimate embrace sent Turvy aiming for the seat of Charlie's trousers.

Camille, a female poodle, was Turvy's mate. She also

enjoyed the run of the home. "She must have read the nursery rhyme about Mary and her little lamb," Charlie said, "because everywhere our Mary goes, Camille is sure to be close behind. One morning she did follow her to school!"

Camille loved to chase anyone who dared to walk by the house. She would go for women's stockings and men's pants. It got so bad that a local retailer complained, "First my poor mother! Then my brother! Now me!"

Helen was told that the man, who was Jewish, believed the MacArthurs were anti-Semitic and that they encouraged their dog to assault his family. She was hurt and annoyed. Molly Picon, the star of the Yiddish stage, laughed at this notion. "Helen is no more anti-Semitic than I am," she said. "She is one of the most democratic persons I know. Why, the greatest compliment I ever received was when I was called 'the Jewish Helen Hayes.' "

When Helen was told about Molly's new nickname, she instantly said, "Well, from now on I'm going to claim that I'm the 'shiksa Molly Picon.' "

Still, she felt that she had an obligation to cure Camille of her nasty habit. "I heard of a dog psychologist," Helen said, "who had been successful with Walter Lippmann's pet. He had a similar problem, only he attacked editors."

After listening to the actress's account of Camille's misdeeds, the animal expert was certain she could remedy the situation. Her solution was to hide in the shubbery armed with a BB gun loaded with paper pellets. She planned on stinging the dog slightly each time she attacked passersby.

However, the instant the woman concealed herself in the bushes, Camille would cuddle close to her and ignore everybody else, but as soon as she left, Camille resumed her nip-and-run assaults.

Christmas was a big event in the MacArthur home. Everybody—even the dogs—participated, sometimes against their wishes. One extremely frigid Yuletide, Mary felt that hot Ovaltine should be left for Santa Claus. Actress Ruth Gordon was visiting at the time. "After we put the finishing touches on the tree," she recalled, "I suddenly remembered Mary's request. Quickly, Charlie filled a cup with steaming Ovaltine, swished it around a couple of times and then drained it. To make it look more authentic he yanked some white hairs from one of the poodles. The animal howled. Charlie soothed him and said happily, 'Now, Mary will think Old Nick left some of his whiskers behind.' "

In the late 1930s Charlie and his wife decided that they should visit Europe once again before "Hitler gobbles it all up." The children were left behind with their governesses and Helen's mother. The MacArthurs were always concerned about leaving Mary and Jamie at home. Whenever they were traveling, they made nightly telephone calls. "At what it's costing," Charlie said, "it would have been cheaper to have them along. But I wonder if kids really want to see museums and stuff like that? I wonder if I do?"

It was an unforgettable trip. In Austria they were invited to stay at a handsome sixteenth-century castle at which touring royalty was often accommodated. The Duke of Kent, another guest, sent word that he was eager to meet Miss Hayes and would be pleased if she and her husband joined him for brandy. Helen had already prepared for bed and said to Charlie, "Tell the duke that I've retired." Then she added flippantly, "If the duke wants to see me, he can very well come here."

Five minutes later MacArthur and the duke appeared at the side of Helen's bed. The duke was beaming and balancing three snifters of brandy on a tray. She was lying with the blankets pulled to her chin, her hair in curlers, and her face covered with cold cream. After the duke had left, she snapped at her husband, "I was never more embarrassed in my life!"

Charlie, who seemed delighted with what he had done, said cheerfully, "At least you didn't have to curtsy."

They visited the village of Hullicourt in France, where Private MacArthur had bivouacked during World War I. Although Charlie's hair was a bit thinner and he had put on some weight, the townspeople recognized him. "*Charlot le formidable* 'as return," they shouted joyfully. They pounded his back and kissed him. Helen listened as they recalled the merriment he had brought to the drab war years. Once MacArthur had dressed a two-hundred-pound hog in a uniform belonging to his commanding officer. Another time he felt that a 10 P.M. curfew was much too early and persuaded the bell ringer at the church to pull the rope ten times when it was actually midnight.

In London they were entertained by the Marchioness of Milford Haven, whose grandmother was Queen Victoria. Helen asked her if Victoria, who had a German background, spoke English with an accent. The marchioness, also of German extraction, looked shocked. "Ach, no," she said. "She het no more eggzent dan you or me!"

Back home, Helen made arrangements to appear in *Ladies and Gentlemen,* a play Charlie and Ben Hecht had written expressly for her. It was the only stage vehicle MacArthur ever completed for his wife. "He was forever coming over to my house with dazzling ideas about writing a play for her," said Hecht. "He'd start, get to page ten, and then stop, shouting, 'It's not nearly good enough for Helen!' Then he'd tear it up and go off to play ice hockey at Petersen's frozen shipyard.

"People are forever asking me, 'Why, did Charlie always need a collaborator?' The answer is quite simple. Writing is a very lonely business. Charlie, who was very affable, loved company; he always needed someone to talk to. He didn't really need a collaborator. He was a marvelous writer, a genius at dialogue. Too bad the critics didn't realize how good he was."

Some did. "*Ladies and Gentlemen* is a rather complicated play," said one reviewer. "There are three love triangles interwoven in the contemporary plot. Miss Hayes is one of these 'other women.' She deserves something better. However, she comes out with some crackerjack lines, undoubtedly courtesy of MacArthur, who is her devoted husband."

Although the play ran on Broadway for many months, Charlie and Ben had reservations about it. "The play's saving grace," said Hecht, "is Helen."

After viewing one performance, Charlie remarked, "As usual my wife is terrific. But the play has a great deal wrong with it. Playwrights, like doctors, should never have anything professionally to do with women they're married to."

He had vowed that he would never return to the film capital. However, the financial blandishments were much too great to ignore. For $50,000 he began commuting to the West Coast to write the scenario for *Gunga Din*.

Donald Ogden Stewart said, "Although their *Gunga Din* script eventually worked out pretty well, there never was a more ludicrous Hollywood assignment. Imagine putting those two on a movie about British imperialism? They were always for the underdog. One of the preliminary scripts was turned back with the notation: 'You just don't seem to understand the white man's burden.' To which Ben and Charlie wrote back, 'The white man's burden seems to be making lots of money. Since we're both white, how about an advance of $20,000?' "

During this stint on the coast MacArthur, Hecht, and John Barrymore were involved in a drinking bout that Hollywood still remembers with awe. Melvin Gordon, a retired studio executive, recounted, "That unholy threesome started out in Barrymore's house, where they drank up all his liquor. Everything. And believe me, that was a lot. Then they went to the place that Charlie and Ben shared. There they did more guzzling. Three sheets to the wind, they managed to crawl to the corner of Hollywood and Vine, where they created a traffic tie-up that lasted for hours. They stopped all the automobiles and demanded tribute—liquor flasks. They were finally led away by the police. But not until traffic was stalled for miles. The next day Charlie and

Ben resumed writing as if nothing had happened."

"Charlie always had a soft spot for his good friend John Barrymore," said Nunnally Johnson. "They were drinking buddies and possessed the same sort of prankish humor, which was encouraged by hoisting a few. Charlie loved to talk about his friend's notorious binges." Johnson was so intrigued with one of them that he and MacArthur decided it would make a splendid plot for a play. It seems that suddenly one night, after five Scotch-and-sodas, Barrymore remembered that he had a teenaged daughter named Diana. From his estranged wife, the poet Michael Strange, he learned that Diana was attending a boarding school near Baltimore, Maryland.

" 'He felt the poor child needed a father's love,' Charlie told me, 'that he wanted to set things straight. So off to the school he goes. Diana refuses to speak to him. But the headmistress is so struck with the lecherous actor, she showers him with adoration. He is so enchanted by her hero worship that he decides to remain at the school indefinitely.' And that's how *Stag at Bay* was born."

Unfortunately, Charlie and Johnson had great difficulty in completing the play. They wrote fifteen different versions and were dissatisfied with each one. "But that didn't stop Charlie from having casting ideas," recalled Johnson. "He approached Fredric March to do the lead, Ingrid Bergman to play the young girl, Josh Logan to do the directing. It never came off because we lost the script—all fifteen of them!" (Years later the theatre department of the Florida State University discovered one of the copies and produced the play.)

Helen and the children visited MacArthur in California. His wife's stage reputation had now made her a major celebrity. Well-known movie stars competed for her presence at their parties. One Saturday night she was again a guest at the palatial home of Joan Crawford. Jamie remembers that he spent the night there. "I shared a room with Joan's son, Christopher," he said. "When it came time for bed, a maid, on orders from her mistress, strapped him to the bedposts so that he couldn't possibly get out and disturb his mother. Although I was pretty young at the time, I was shocked. Was that the way they treated children in Hollywood? I thought how lucky I was—my parents wouldn't do that to me in a million years."

Shortly after *Gunga Din* was completed, Sam Goldwyn called "the two cutdowns" into his office. "Now, what new ideas have you Katzenjammer Kids got for me?" he inquired.

They didn't have anything, but Hecht began to tell him about an opium den in the London Limehouse district that was infested with real snakes. At this point Charlie reached for his hat and coat and edged to a window. As Ben switched the scene of the projected scenario to the Brazilian jungle, MacArthur put his hat and coat on and opened the window. Hecht was talking about rustlers and sheriffs when Charlie climbed onto the ledge. A terrified Goldwyn and a languid Hecht managed to pull him to safety.

When he was back on firm ground, Charlie said solemnly. "Sam, I've got it! A frustrated insurance salesman bets the company's money on a fixed race. But the horse breaks a leg and the poor fellow tries to end it all by jumping out of a window. He's rescued in the nick of time by a kind soul."

Later, MacArthur spoke about the jumping episode to actor Reginald Gardiner. "To keep your sanity in this place," he said, "it's very necessary to put on your hat and coat and leave the earth at least once every fortnight."

Hats and coats figured prominently in another MacArthur frolic. It happened when Helen said that she would prepare a turkey for Thanksgiving. Although normally a good cook, she said to Charlie and Jim, "If I happen to ruin it, I don't want to hear any complaints from either of you. We'll just get up without saying a word and go out to a restaurant for our holiday dinner!"

After a great deal of time and exertion in the kitchen, she triumphantly carried the stuffed bird into the dining room. The male MacArthurs were sitting in silence—with their hats and coats on.

Charlie was delighted to make his son a partner in crime. Once in the course of a vacation in the Caribbean, they engaged a taxi to take them to Bluebeard's Castle, a buccaneer landmark in St. Thomas. On the way there they stopped for lunch and then got back into the waiting cab. After they had gone several miles, Helen suddenly realized that she had left her eyeglasses in the restaurant. They returned to the restaurant, where she got out to retrieve them.

As soon as she exited, father and son got into a quick huddle. With Charlie shouting directions, Jim emerged from the taxi and ran after his mother. Helen was in the cocktail lounge asking the bartender about her lost glasses. That was when Jim burst in yelling, "Please! Please! Don't give my mother another drink!"

11

"I Didn't Raise My Child to Be an Actor, but..."

Helen has stated repeatedly that she and Charlie did not encourage Mary and Jamie to choose the life of the theatre. She would often tell them how attractive other fields were. "Rather hoped it would take," she said. But she discovered that it is difficult for a mother to speak disparagingly of a profession when her children have grown up watching her enjoy being an actress.

"I suppose, if the truth be known, we showed our pride when they performed," Helen said. "I guess we encouraged them to exhibit their talents. Half a century ago it was common practice to have one's daughter play her latest piano selection for company and have one's son recite "The Charge of the Light Brigade" in the parlor after dinner. With electronic entertainment, that went out of fashion. But as an actress and mother I feel that we ought once again to invite our children to entertain us—to read aloud, act, play the piano and to learn to express themselves in front of others. What better way to teach them confidence and composure."

When Mary and Jamie were very young, Helen made up a series of stories she called *The Further Adventures of Minnie Weisenpfeffer.* "The children loved them," Helen said. "One day Mary got up on her feet and, using the same thriller-chiller inflections that I did, retold the tales to Charlie and me. We burst into applause. We had been genuinely entertained."

Two days before her seventh birthday Mary made her debut in the last scene of *Victoria Regina*, in which as young Princess Ena Battenburg, she walked on but spoke no lines. However, she quickly caught the volatile impact from the audience and from backstage. Her parents and their friends felt she had given a silent but smashing premier performance. Noel Coward sent her a large bouquet of roses; Gilbert Miller, the play's producer, gave her a jar of pecan sugar cakes, and Vincent Price bought her a gold watch.

"It was after midnight when she returned home," Charlie recalled. "She should have been sleepy. Instead, she suddenly shouted, 'I didn't get paid!' "

Later, when the show went on tour, Mary made further appearances. She told friends about her experiences. "No one bothers about being very polite," she said. "The company seemed to split up into three groups. The singles—most of these were elderly and with double chins. And there were those that played poker continuously. The third group was known as the 'Grand Group.' They behaved on the train as if they were sitting in the throne room at Buckingham Palace. It all sounds crazy, but it really was a wonderful life. More like going away to private school. You make a whole mess of new friends. And then when the show closes for the last time, everybody sings *Auld Lang Syne.*"

Jamie made his theatrical bow when he was eight and a half years old. That summer, Mary, who was by then working with an Olney, Maryland, stock company, invited him for a visit. He discovered they needed a young boy for a part in *The Corn Is Green.* Helen permitted him to try out for the role. He was hired. For two weeks Jamie played a Welsh laddie. The part was twelve lines long and all in Welsh.

He actually made his first public appearance at an earlier age. His mother was touring with *Harriet.* Jamie was backstage during a performance when he heard her say, "My son! Where is my son?" Jamie did not realize it was a line from the play and rushed to her side, yelling, "Mommie! Here I am!"

Roger Kostmayer, a boyhood friend, said, "I suppose if I had thought about it I would have realized Jim—he felt the name Jamie was too babyish—would wind up acting. With a heritage like that, what else? But we were too busy getting into trouble to occupy our minds with the future. He was pretty much of a hell-raiser. We spent lots of time in the principal's office. His parents would fret, but I always suspected that his father was secretly pleased.

"When Jim and I broke windows with baseballs or were caught smoking ordinary cigarettes—that's all kids did in those days—instead of punishing us, Charlie would listen solemnly and then begin to tell us wild stories about things he did when he was a boy. He talked to us as equals. Helen did some of the same. She never talked down. I felt that most of the time she was quite relaxed with Jim. The few exceptions were when my mother called her from time to time to report that he was tossing rocks at street lamps. She'd quickly come to pick him up. 'Whatever am I going to do with him?' she'd say exasperatedly as he got in the car. But the next day when I visited their home it all seemed forgotten."

Mary and her brother spent many exhilarating hours backstage, listening to their mother speak of the theatre. Helen frequently had some very definite thoughts about actors and acting:

On the demands of stardom:

There are many times when the duties of being a star seem to outweigh the advantages. Too often stardom means gilded slavery. It helps to be prepared for it—to realize it's a form of wondrous strange slavery.

On learning lines:

It's hard, tedious work. The time comes when you hate every word of the play and you wonder how you got into it. Yet, I firmly believe that there is no such thing as a "poor study" in the theatre—the actor who can't memorize lines. I think that the only time you can't memorize is when you refuse to face up to the deadly grind of study.

On role-playing:

Childbirth is easy compared to giving birth to a role in a play. There is nothing more difficult in the theatre than undertaking a part. I have found that it helps tremendously to fully understand and almost fall in love with the character. I've always—well, nearly always—agreed to appear in a play because the character I would portray caught my imagination.

On duty:
There are too many actors who have mistaken ideas about artistic integrity. They believe the truth has to be vulgar, depressing and ugly. Nonsense. Life is so often beautiful. The main duty of a player is to play. To use your talents to the limit of your capacity.

On good diction:
The most valuable advice I ever received was to read Shakespeare aloud. Now I pass it on. Anyone who wants to improve the way he speaks should do the same.

On the need for solitude:
Society can often be very tense. Therefore, it's so very necessary for the actor to find time to be alone. To watch the waves break. To look at snowcapped mountain peaks. Almost to observe the grass grow.

On logic:
Theatregoers come not only to anticipate the unexpected, but come to expect it. When the curtain goes up, logic quickly turns into illogic. Black becomes white, white becomes black. However, it's all very much the same. John is still John, even if he's now called Jane.

On fame:
Whenever I think I'm getting a swelled head, I remember John Golden, the famous producer, telling me how wonderful and well known I was. "Can't you just visualize your name being used for a theatre?" he said. Then he spelled out, "H-e-l-e-n H-a-y-s." That missing *e* continues to deflate my ego.*

*Many years later, to celebrate her half century devotion to the stage, a Broadway theatre was renamed in her honor. This time the spelling was correct.

"Helen's stage tips to her children must have rubbed off on them," said Marc Connelly. "I'm certain that if Mary had lived, she would have one day rivaled her mother. As for Jim, Helen's elated by his acting talent. I remember once when he made an appearance on some television show, she told me, 'He's so very good.' She seemed to glow out loud—and with Helen that feat is quite possible."

12
Major MacArthur Goes to War

Early in 1941, when it looked as though the United States would surely enter World War II, Charlie volunteered his services. He was told to inform the public about the need to resist the Nazis. He and Ben Hecht wrote the script for one of New York's biggest, most emotional, political pageants. It was performed at the eighteen-thousand-seat Madison Square Garden.

"Everybody begged for tickets," recalled Billy Rose, the show's producer. "Half of the city's cops were needed to keep order. Dozens of fire engines were at the ready. It was sheer pandemonium."

The memorable extravaganza was called *Fun to Be Free*. History may well consider it America's opening anti-Nazi shot. It convinced many people that, one way or another, they had to go to war. Henry L. Stimson, Roosevelt's secretary of war, personally thanked the authors. "Our country is in your debt," he told them.

Stimson's gratitude was not sufficient to satisfy Charlie. He desperately wanted to enlist as a private and stated his wish in a flood of strongly worded letters. "Get me back in the trenches," he pleaded. When told that modern warfare no longer used that type of shelter, he replied, "Now, I can see how badly I'm needed to show you how it's done!"

MacArthur's age and poor physical condition caused by heavy drinking ruled out any possibility of his becoming an ordinary GI. Sulkily, he sought a commission. When he was asked by the general who interviewed him what his reaction would be to becoming an officer, he replied truthfully, "One of complete confusion."

"If we made you one, what rank do you think you should have?"

"I should at the very least be made a fort."

"I'm sorry. We already have a Fort MacArthur. It's in southern California."

"Then how about a general?"

"We also have a General MacArthur."

Charlie was commissioned a major in the Chemical Warfare Service. When knowledge of the appointment reached his friends, Nunnally Johnson blurted, "My God! Aren't they afraid he'll drink it all up?"

Screenwriter Herman J. Mankiewicz, a former newspaper critic, predicted that MacArthur would be the Chemical Corp's chief weapon. "They'll fly over Berlin holding him head over heels," he said. "Then when he breathes on the German capital, it will collapse."

The army may have failed to make use of Charlie's intemperance, but he managed to participate in several raids over Berlin and tossed empty whiskey bottles on the city. Larry Monnarino, a former B-52 bombardier, spoke of some of Charlie's shenanigans. "He conned us into taking him along on one of our missions. He told us he was an observer for General Montgomery. When we asked him why Montgomery didn't send an English officer, he had a ready answer. 'My father was born in Great Britain,' he replied, 'and, I, myself, drink Scotch.' With a response like that, we figured, he had to be kosher. That was until we got over Berlin. Right at that point he opened his knapsack and handed me a mess of bottles stuffed with toilet tissue. 'Drop them on the German high command,' he said.

"On the return trip one of the guys hauled out a harmonica and started playing. MacArthur said that his wife was a harmonica virtuoso. And that when she played he did a soft-shoe routine. Then right in front of us in the bomb bay of the rocking plane, which was dodging flak, he started dancing. The plane suddenly dived and he fell flat on his fanny. He got up, smiled and dusted himself off. 'Fortunately,' he said, 'that's my least vulnerable spot.' He resumed his dancing."

Charlie was promoted to lieutenant-colonel. He traveled to other war areas as assistant to the chief of Chemical Warfare and liaison between civilian scientists and the military. To ensure first-class service, he filled out the "person to notify" space on his passport with the name of Harry S. Truman. "This worked wonders," MacArthur confided. "Officials the world over practically fell on their beaks trying to be helpful."

In Agrai, India, Charlie somehow arrived at a native market near the Taj Mahal. For 5 rupees he bought Helen a love flower that was guaranteed to cure an aching heart. In London, after telling an immigration officer that he was Truman's illegitimate half-brother, he introduced Clark Gable to Bea Lillie. It was soon apparent that the Hollywood leading man and the British star were very interested in each other. MacArthur said slyly, "Alec [Woollcott] would be proud of my matchmaking."

Shortly after D day, Charlie made an appearance at the front. Journalist Quentin Reynolds, who was also there, recalled, "He was an inspiration to our fighting men. I know it's hard to think of him as a father figure, but that's exactly what he was—a zany, mixed-up, lovable dad. The kind those boys wished they had. One morning he showed up with loaves of nut bread, cognac, jelly beans, and a whole slew of exotic fruit. I believe they were papayas, mangos, and kumquats. Where he got them I'll never know. He winked and said, 'I've been to war before!' "

Charlie's sympathy always rested with the enlisted man. He became a co-conspirator with a corporal who had just finished a four-week training course at the Chemical Warfare School in Edgewood Arsenal, Maryland. The soldier, Edward Graham, a former divinity student from Carson City, Nevada, and Charlie often engaged in Scripture contests. MacArthur, who as a child had been punished for a wrong answer, was rarely stumped.

The corporal told Charlie that he objected to the motto of the school: *Elementis Proelium Regamus* ("Let Us Rule the Battle by Means of the Elements"). MacArthur promptly helped Graham compose a letter to authorities in Washington that demanded an immediate change. "Our Latin may be faulty, but our advice isn't. Better change it to read: *Elementis Abdomenac Exultae Regnua*—'Let Us Rule the Battle by Means of Belly Dancers.' " A postscript was added: "Beware of *Hebrews*

7:12—'Of necessity a *change* also of the law.' And *Matthew* 23:14—'Woe unto you, scribes and Pharisees, hypocrites . . . ye shall receive the greater damnation.' "

They never received an answer.

Charlie learned that one of the brass's favorite slogans was RHIP—Rank Has Its Privileges. This time he used the telephone to suggest a change of phrase. RHIP, he proposed, should stand for Raises Help Indigent Privates!

While his military duties took him to Europe and Asia, Helen also participated in the war effort. Several years before, the MacArthurs had purchased a thirty-acre farm near Nyack. "Now, with Charlie serving in the army, I was determined to work it and become self-sufficient," Helen said. "I wanted to have enough produce left over to sell. However, as a farmer I was spectacularly unsuccessful."

The war had drained off most local labor, so that the actress, her secretary, the two children, her son's nurse, and a young friend of Mary's did most of the planting and cultivating. Helen was appearing in *Harriet*, a historical play about Harriet Beecher Stowe, who wrote *Uncle Tom's Cabin.*

Four evenings a week, at exactly 6 P.M., she would leave the farm and head for the theatre. To save gasoline, she would travel by bus, changing at the George Washington Bridge to the subway. She also managed to make many appearances at war-bond rallies and to work at the Stage Door and the Merchant Seaman's canteens.

On the days Helen would return to the farm, her secretary, Margaret English, called for her at the theatre.

Before leaving the country, Ms. English would load the station wagon up with fresh eggs so that Helen could sell them to members of the cast. Tallulah Bankhead, who was a Rockland County neighbor, estimated that the eggs cost Helen about a dollar apiece. "She had the most pampered hens I've ever seen," said Miss Bankhead. "Why, she even covered them with silk quilts on cold nights!"

Another farm product that Helen sold was strawberries. She and Ms. English stuffed them into small boxes and peddled them door to door. "This was a more profitable venture," said Tallulah. "Helen only lost 50 cents on a box!"

Mildred Eisenstadt, a costume designer, who also lived nearby, was a regular customer. "Helen," she recalled, "seemed lots happier when someone bought her eggs and strawberries than she was when enthusiastic audiences insisted she take an extra curtain call. One time she told me, 'I feel that every egg I sell brings my Charlie closer to home. By the way would you like to buy some freshly picked tomatoes?' "

Helen's energetic work on the farm led to an acute case of bursitis in her right shoulder. She was hospitalized unwillingly. *Harriet* had to shut down for a month. But as soon as she recovered, she returned to the play. She had again excited reviewers in this play. Lewis Nichols of the *New York Times* called her portrayal of Harriet Beecher Stowe a "masterpiece." Howard Barnes of the *New York Herald Tribune* regarded her characterization "luminous."

Harriet ran for 377 performances, closing down just before election day. That's when Helen startled her friends by endorsing Republican Thomas E. Dewey for

President. "How could a woman make so daffy a decision," wondered Richard Maney, who handled publicity for the show.

"I know I should keep my mouth shut," she told him. "But I'm convinced that Dewey would end the war and bring Charlie home. I fear that is my number-one priority. And I'll do anything to achieve it!"

"I did believe it," said Maney. "She wasn't responding as a celebrity, but as a concerned citizen—as the wife of a serviceman. Party lines were never something to bother Helen Hayes. In the 1944 congressional campaign she joined her neighbors Ben Hecht and Maxwell Anderson in denouncing archconservative Congressman Hamilton Fish, Sr. She listed herself as a 'Republican for Bennet'—Fish's Democratic opponent. She contended that Fish was against preparedness, against the draft, against lend-lease. When Fish said, 'As a politician, Miss Hayes is a good actress, she replied, 'As a politician, Mr. Fish is a bad actor.' Charlie heard about her rebuttal and was delighted. 'See what I taught her?' he said."

Maney felt that it was very easy to tell when Helen received a letter from her husband. "She would waltz into the theatre," he recalled, "and practically sing a chorus with her ever-present eggs-for-sale. One evening she was positively flushed with joy. She told me that Charlie had just sent her a package from India. It contained a handful of uncut emeralds. The accompanying card read, 'I wish they were peanuts.' "

Returning home from World War II—his third war—Charlie was temporarily very quiet. His reunion with Helen and the children was marked by embarrassed silence. He told Ben Hecht that World War I was a farce compared to this one. "In that fight the bloodletting was more like tomato ketchup thrown from the wings of stage left."

MacArthur's youth, his remarkable capacity for detachment, and his ability always to remain calm skidded him through World War I. "Now," said Hecht, "it was all different. He seemed overwhelmed by the senselessness of the killing and destruction. He'd write frequent passages about how simple and kind the world should be. Then he'd rip them out of his typewriter and send them sailing on the river."

When Charlie got back into lively male company, there were the expected demands for humorous war tales. He was never one to disappoint anybody intentionally. His reminiscences about General Eisenhower were affectionate but somewhat irreverent. Eisenhower was then "just an easygoing brass. In North Africa he could have had the bellies of the best belly dancers. But all he wanted was a Kansas City steak hangover!"

Charlie admired General Patton's gallantry, his smash-bang tactics. He told his friends, "Why, Patton would have made a damned good *Herald-Examiner* reporter. He refuses to take no for an answer!"

13

The Death of Mary

"**I'**m sure that there is nothing harder for a mother than to survive her own child," said Barbara Boll Herndon, who was one of Mary's closest friends. She was the daughter of a Nyack neighbor and had met Mary in the sixth grade. "For ma'am—I've always called Helen that—and for Charlie, too, it was the end of the world. They loved her so. And she them."

Mary and Barbara were inseparable. "When we were in our early teens we made a pact," recalled Barbara. "The first one of us to have a daughter would be named after the other. My Mary has a most glorious namesake. Mary MacArthur was everything you hope your child will be—pretty, intelligent, talented, and at ease with everybody. A real supergirl."

In the summer of 1949, nineteen-year-old Mary MacArthur and her mother appeared together in *Good Housekeeping*, a three-act comedy by William McCleery. The Theatre Guild was planning to bring it to Broadway. It scheduled one of the tryouts in Westport,

Connecticut, a town with a handy beach fifty-five miles from New York City.

During the out-of-town run Mary did not feel too well. She refused to admit it and secretly swallowed aspirins between the acts. She finally said that she was a little tired. Helen quickly summoned a doctor. He examined Mary and said that there was nothing to worry about. "Just a slight touch of flu," he reported comfortingly.

Despite his reassurance, Helen insisted that Mary go home for a brief rest. She wanted to accompany her daughter, but Mary pressured her into staying with the show. "We can't have two members of the family leave the cast," she said. "If you don't promise to remain, I won't leave!"

Shirley Standlee, who was hastily moved up into Mary's role, recalled her waving good-bye and telling everyone that she would be right back. "She was a trouper if there ever was one," Ms. Standlee said. "Even though Helen Hayes was her mother, she never put on airs. Why, it was not unusual to find her sweeping up the dressing room."

At the time, Charlie was being treated for an ulcer at at New York's Lenox Hill Hospital. He and Helen were relieved when a second doctor also said that Mary's fatigue was caused by the flu. Aureomycin was prescribed. It did not help. She grew worse. A new diagnosis was made: Mary had bulbar polio.

Helen charged into the hospital just as her daughter was placed in an iron lung across the hall from her father. Charlie left his sick bed to join his wife in a twenty-four-hour vigil. Their daughter tried to smile at them as she wiggled her toes and fingers to prove she could move. Charlie, who had not prayed in years, clasped his hands and wept.

Mary remained in the iron lung. She died several days later. Helen, who had always prided herself on being stoic, broke down. Over and over she wailed, "God, why her?" Charlie was silent. He ran out of the hospital and aimlessly walked the streets most of that night.

Jim, who was eleven years old at the time, was too young to understand the full meaning of death. He said, "I only knew I felt miserable along with Mom and Pop. I loved Mary but not in the special way that they did." He remembers his mother saying to him, "You'll have to look after your father now!" And Charlie pushing him into a corner and whispering, "You'll have to take care of Mom now!"

A brief, private funeral service conducted by the Reverend Dr. William Neely Ross, former pastor of the Dutch Reformed Church, was held at the Oak Hill Cemetery in Nyack. It was attended only by immediate relatives and a few of Mary's friends. There were no flowers. Charlie and Helen asked instead that donations be sent instead to the National Foundation for Infantile Paralysis.

Hundreds of people sent their condolences. General Dwight D. Eisenhower wrote about losing his first born, a boy of three. Claire Booth Luce reminded the MacArthurs of how she, too, had her daughter taken from her at age nineteen. Mrs. Theodore Roosevelt described her feelings when she learned her son Quentin had been killed.

"When we heard the beautiful and talented Mary MacArthur had died," said Josh Logan, "Nedda [his wife] and I rushed to Helen's house. Helen had always been small; but that night she was shriveled, shrunk, pitiful. The day after the funeral Charlie called and said, 'Josh, you've got to save Helen. You must put her in a play—and quick!' "

Barbara Herndon recalled, "We were worried about ma'am's sanity. 'I cannot stand the torture of going on,' she kept repeating. Yet, in many ways I felt that Charlie was the hardest hit by Mary's death. But even though he was still sick himself, he managed to offer his wife some of the strength she so badly needed."

A stranger telephoned the apartment. MacArthur answered. The caller said that his young son had just died of polio. He desperately wanted to know if he could bring his wife to talk to Helen. "At first I flatly refused," the actress said. " 'I can't!' I wailed. Charlie, always very sensitive, thought it might help. The couple came. Right off I realized that the wife felt her effort would aid her husband. He, in turn, thought she would be helped. I could tell they were playing some kind of a game because they loved each other so much. Like Charlie and myself, they were bereft."

MacArthur pressured his wife to accept the lead in *The Wysteria Trees*, a play Logan had especially selected for her. It was based on Chekhov's *The Cherry Orchard*. At first Helen refused. "I can't possibly go on," she insisted. Instead, the MacArthurs went to a secluded ranch in New Mexico. Then they traveled to California and Hawaii.

In Honolulu, Charlie did a curious thing. "I was out walking alone," he later told Marc Connelly. "A pair of sunglasses in the window of a sports store appealed to me. I thought they'd be just right for Mary, so I went in and bought them. I was outside the store when it suddenly hit me—Mary was dead. All at once the bag started burning my fingers. Yet, somehow I couldn't toss it away. Just then I noticed a girl about Mary's age. Without saying a word, I thrust the glasses into her hands and ran off. I never told Helen about it. How could I? It would have been more than she could possibly bear. Those two were so close!"

All the traveling did not help. When they returned to Nyack, Charlie mentioned *The Wysteria Trees* again. This time Helen agreed to give it a try. As he had hoped, she was soon becoming caught up in learning lines and building a character. "She doesn't have time to think of anything but the play," he told Logan. She worked hard. It opened on Broadway in six weeks. As usual her notices were excellent.

But "Helen was still very disconsolate," said Elaine Whitelaw, a vice-president of the March of Dimes Foundation. "Another member of the organization and myself sent her a letter of sympathy. We were invited to see her in the New York apartment. After making some small talk, I asked her if she would be our national chairman of volunteers. She accepted. Her first job was to speak at a polio conference in Washington, D.C. When she stepped to the podium, the audience, which had been somewhat fidgety, suddenly became very quiet. No one moved. No one coughed. She spoke so softly, so movingly. She was given a standing ovation when she said, 'We won't stop until polio is eliminated everywhere!'

"In those days Charlie would not accompany his wife to any rallies. I felt that he didn't want to see anybody who was associated with polio. One afternoon I was sitting with Helen at the apartment. We had become good friends. I said that I owed her husband a real debt of thanks. My young daughter had refused to do any reading, but after she saw his movie *Wuthering Heights*, she wanted to know if there was a book about it. 'She's been reading ever since,' I boasted elatedly. Helen made me repeat the story to Charlie.

" 'Are you sure it wasn't the star of the movie, Laurence Olivier, that intrigued her?' he asked. But it was apparent that he was pleased. From that point we got on very well. A few weeks later he arranged a radio show for the March of Dimes. He got a large group of theatrical personalities to lend their talents. Stars like Gertrude Lawrence, Lunt and Fontanne, Beatrice Lillie, David Niven. It was an absolutely breathtaking hour."

Yet, Helen was still restless. "Does a mother ever get over losing a child?" she asked. "I kept wondering if I had done anything wrong? Where did I fail?" On Sundays, when there were no performances, she would prowl the Nyack woods or pace beside the river, reliving the past. Often she visited the local cemetery where Mary was buried. Charlie had composed an inscription for his daughter's gravestone: "Here beneath this stone doth lie / As much beauty as could die."

"And then one day," Helen realized that "I had been lost in the material world. Now, I suddenly knew that God wanted me to help others."

"She became a ball of fire on our behalf," said Ms. Whitelaw. "All I ever had to do was pick up the phone and call her. She was never too busy to visit bereaved parents. She'd spend hours with them. Dr. Jonas Salk says her tremendous zeal spurred him on."

Victoria Loomis was one of the mothers Helen visited. "Miss Hayes was on tour in some play. I forget the name. Anyway, when it opened in Washington, she came to see me. My little daughter had just died from poliomyelitis. She was only seven years old when she passed away. I was in terrible shape. I was sure that my husband and friends thought I was going crazy with grief. That's when Miss Hayes came to see me. I'll bless her until I draw my final breath. She talked to me for a long, long time and gave me the will to go on. A year later I had another child, a six-pound, eight-ounce, blue-eyed girl. My husband and I named her Helen Hayes Loomis."

14

"30" for Charlie

In newspaper parlance, the figure 30 signifies the end of a story as it rips out of a typewriter or clatters from a teletype. MacArthur once confided to Donald Ogden Stewart that he hoped the obituary above his 30 would make interesting reading. "Do you think it will?" he asked plaintively.

"At the time, I simply nodded," Stewart recalled. "I didn't want to discuss death, especially his. I was afraid to tell him how entertaining his obit would be. Except, who could write it but himself? He was a unique man. Genuine as Tiffany diamonds or Milwaukee beer.

"I've often asked myself what Charlie's special magic was. He wasn't the greatest journalist ever, nor the greatest playwright. But he was perceptive; he could spot a phony at a glance. He was a fearless inconoclast. He was a philosopher who could accept evil and be compassionate. He knew how to laugh, love, and have a lark. And he changed a part of this world for the better."

Dramatists often borrowed MacArthur's personality. Thorton Wilder modeled his hero for *Heaven Is My Destination* after Charlie. F. Scott Fitzgerald put him in *Tender Is the Night*, S. N. Behrman freely admitted that *No Time for Comedy* is chiefly about him, Moss Hart wrote him into *Merrily We Roll Along*. In Hollywood, directors and producers would order their writers, "Make the hero a MacArthur! Loving, cynical, compassionate, hard-drinking, hell-raising, and damning."

Charlie lived seven years after Mary died, but Helen said he faded from the moment he knew his daughter was gone. His contract with life had been torn up. His creative ability floundered. Helplessly his wife watched her Charlie die.

There were short intervals when he would briefly shake off his despair and resume the role of the happy-go-lucky man-about-town. He and Helen were invited to appear on Edward R. Murrow's "Person to Person" television show. When the CBS commentator wanted to know MacArthur's philosophy of life, Charlie quickly replied, "A condemned man whose hanging I once covered in Chicago summed it up in four words. As the prisoner reached the gallows steps he asked, 'Is this thing safe?' "

The MacArthurs had let Nunnally Johnson borrow their house for his wedding. Mary had been the flower girl and nearly stolen the show.

"My bride forgave her," Nunnally said. "Who could not? She had her mother's poise and her father's merry eyes and she looked so lovely coming down the aisle that I admit I almost married her by mistake."

Johnson remembered a lunch in a converted old

speakeasy a few months after Mary died. "Charlie," he recalled, "sat in a corner, looking sullenly at the opposite wall. We ordered conventional plates of roast beef and mashed potatoes and ate wordlessly. Then from the next table we overheard a man boasting and dropping big names. 'I know him . . . I was saying to her . . .

"Well, if there was anything Charlie detested it was bragging. There was a mess of uneaten mashed potatoes on his plate. He loaded a pile on a tablespoon and snapped it right at the man's bald head. I was fascinated as I saw it land on target.

" 'Oops, sorry,' Charlie apologized sweetly. Then he leaned closer to me. 'I taught Mary that trick,' he whispered and then he wept."

MacArthur developed a cataract in one of his eyes. A stomach ulcer signaled recurrent trouble. He drank earlier in the day. Some of his friends now avoided him because they could not bear to watch his anguish.

Charlie realized that his wife was turning down theatrical offers in order to be at his side. He kept urging her to say yes. Hollywood director Leo McCarey begged her to make a movie for him. After a great deal of coaxing, Helen returned to the film capital. She agreed to play the older lead in McCarey's *My Son John*. It was a movie about Communist subversion in America. Robert Walker was cast as her traitor-offspring. When asked why she finally accepted the role, she replied that she and Charlie had read about the trials of the American Communists and wondered how the parents of such people felt.

Helen was not very happy about the way she played

Walker's mother in *My Son John*. She called herself "Old Rubber Face." Charlie and the critics disagreed. MacArthur told Hecht, "She improves with age. Just imagine what she'll be like at 103?"

The reviewers were unanimous in their praise: "Touchingly human and beautiful"; "Only Helen Hayes could have done it so movingly"; "A lesson to all actresses who find themselves cast as a grieving mother."

While Helen was making the film, the studio wanted her to write an article about the ten most memorable stage performances she had ever seen. "All my spare time belongs to my husband," she replied rigidly. Charlie, who had also come to Hollywood, convinced her to change her mind. "After all," he said. "I can't have the reading public believe anyone closely associated with me stands in the path of the printed word."

The casual literary assignment took her on a nostalgic trip through all her theatrical experiences. It was news that Helen Hayes was critically reviewing the past performances of her colleagues and rivals. Charlie helped her narrow down the number of shows covered with a graceful preface in which she said that she had played eight shows a week for the last thirty or so years and did not have the opportunity to see all the plays she wanted to. "There are undoubtedly many significant performances that I have missed."

Although she insisted that she was listing them at random, the actor that came to her mind first was John Barrymore in *Hamlet*. It had been many years ago, but she still remembered every detail. For her, Barrymore traded his identity, body and soul, for Shakespeare's Prince of Denmark. "He never lost the poetry of his lines," she said. "And at the same time he didn't put any of them in italics." Helen felt that he played the tragic, tortured prince as Shakespeare intended it.

Next she thought of Laurence Olivier and his shattering portrayal of the king in the Old Vic production of *Oedipus Rex.* She singled out the memorable moment when he learned that his wife was also his mother.

Helen was frankly jealous of Shirley Booth in *Come Back, Little Sheba.* "That's the art of comedy in its most elegant form," she said. "Shirley Booth had complete control of herself, her part, and her audience."

Marlon Brando as Stanley Kowalski in *A Streetcar Named Desire* appeared on the list, but Helen had strong reservations about Brando the man. She felt that he used the theatre unfairly. "He mumbled and muttered," she said, "and he seemed to be doing just about everything he pleased. Not only did he disregard the audience, he also disregarded the author, the director, and practically everyone except himself." Yet she believed he managed to discharge an animal magnetism that was exactly right for the part.

The most extravagant praise was saved for Laurette Taylor in *The Glass Menagerie.* Helen played the lead, Amanda, in the London company. Ever honest, she said, "I believe I did a good job, but in my hands it didn't have the shine that it had in hers. She was transcendent in every role she played."

After one of the performances Helen sent her a fan note: "To Laurette, my guiding star." In acknowledgment Miss Taylor gave her a picture of herself inscribed, "To Helen, who knows how to follow her star." Helen said it was the most prized picture of all she possessed.

Sadie Geller, a studio publicist, felt that the list's final sentence was undoubtedly Charlie's. It read: "If a press agent asks me for another list, to recall the ten *least* memorable performances I've ever seen, then we'll really have something to argue about."

After finishing *My Son John,* Helen left the West Coast for Nyack. Thereafter, the MacArthurs rarely left their home. One of the exceptions was the wedding of Mary's friend, Barbara Boll. "He and ma'am were wonderful guests," Barbara said. "But I had the distinct feeling that when the marriage vows were read, they were both thinking how marvelous it would have been to be present at their daughter's wedding. Ma'am's face always lights up when she thinks of Mary. Charlie became very solemn."

Shortly after the wedding Charlie and Helen donated a Mary MacArthur Scholarship to the American Theatre Wing training program. Then they helped set up the Mary MacArthur Respiratory Unit of the Children's Medical Center. In the Nyack Hospital they established a living memorial to their daughter—a Japanese garden for the patients and their families.

During Charlie's last years, Helen often asked Anita Loos to watch over him when she had to be in the theatre. One evening MacArthur became violently ill. Anita quickly summoned a doctor. The physician was alarmed at his patient's condition and delicately asked him what his religious faith was. Charlie opened one eye. "I'm a phallic worshipper," he said.

When a series of blood transfusions were prescribed,

he told the doctor, "Make sure I get a tap dancer's blood. I've always wanted to be able to kick up my heels." He woke up after one transfusion to find six physicians in white coats surrounding his bed. "What the hell is this?" he demanded. "Some kind of block party?"

He insisted on being released immediately. "If you sawbones vamoose at once," he said, "I promise I'll make you all famous! I'll walk out of here on my own steam. You'll all go down in medical journals as having performed a miracle!"

One of the doctors said, "Let me handle him—I know these Broadway types." And then he told Charlie, "OK, MacArthur, you may leave the hospital. But only under the following conditions: you have to be carried out by four Chinese midgets, followed by a brass band that's led by Mary Martin."

Charlie, as was later reported, waited for the physicians to exit. Then he phoned *Variety* to learn the whereabouts of the Long Trek Sam vaudeville troupe. His next call was to the musician's union to price a three-piece band. Finally, he phoned Mary Martin to ask her when she was free.

"Fortunately," said Ben Hecht, "he was discharged before the hospital authorities had to reckon with that weird-looking ensemble."

Helen was offered the role of the dowager empress of Russia in the 20th Century–Fox movie, *Anastasia*. She turned it down, since it was to be filmed in England. She explained that she did not want to leave Charlie. Instead, she accepted a one-shot appearance in a 1956 television version of *Cradle Song*. However, she had to cancel it when he was readmitted to the hospital. He died the following Saturday. Medical reports listed an intense internal hemorrhage as the cause of death.

Friends disagreed. "Charlie died because of a broken heart," said Hecht. "But even toward the very end his elfish sense of humor didn't desert him. Helen held his hand tightly those last few minutes. She whispered, 'I love you.' Opening his eyes for the final time, he winked and replied, 'You should.'"

Hundreds of notables from the theatre world attended his funeral service, among them Richard Rodgers, Ruth Gordon, Garson Kanin, Oscar Hammerstein II, Beatrice Lillie, Dorothy and Lillian Gish, Irving Berlin, Alfred Lunt, Paul Muni, and Herman Shumlin. Hecht, his longtime friend and collaborator, delivered the eulogy. For a moment it looked as if it would not come off. Just as Hecht prepared to speak, a heavy wreath hanging on a curtain started swaying violently. The mourners were dumbfounded. Was this Charlie's way of nixing any warmhearted words said about him? Hecht smiled knowingly and began the tribute to his dead companion:

"We wrote plays and movies together. But our literary work was only a sideline of our relationship. . . . We remained newspaper reporters and continued to keep our hats on before the boss, drop ashes on the floor, and disclaim all practical people. . . .

"MacArthur was a man of quicker perception than anyone I have ever known. He seemed without psychological attitudes and yet he was as aware of people as if he had eavesdropped on them in an analyst's office. . . . People scampered toward him as if pulled by a magnet. Alec Woollcott, who loved him, said to me once, 'What a perfect world this would be if it were peopled by MacArthurs.' I knew what he meant. It would be a world in which people charmed each other and let each other alone, . . . in which people knew each other's secrets, but never intruded on each other.

"One of the many attractive things about my friend was his modesty. In the years I knew him, I never heard him utter a boast on any subject. . . . His mind grinned at sham. He played tricks on everything pompous. And his heart stayed full of compassion for anyone in pain or misfortune. . . .

"Our lustiest and most high-hearted friend is dead, but the legend of Charles MacArthur will begin to grow now around his fine name. For Charlie was more than a man of talent. He was himself a great piece of writing. His gaiety, wildness, and kindness; his love for his bride, Helen, and his two children and for his clan of brothers and sister; his wit and his adventures will live a long, long while. When he was young, Charlie used to sing a moody Scotch song. It echoes on his death: 'Bonnie Charlie's gone away / Out across the deep blue sea / Many a heart will break in two.' "

15

Helen Carries On Alone

F riends said that with Charlie gone, Helen was devastated. "She was in total confusion," recalled Marc Connelly.

Jim tried to console his grieving mother. "What should have been his carefree days were being spent struggling to make me forget," she said.

Anita Loos, Ruth Gordon, Lillian Gish, and others knew that Helen's rescue lay in acting. They urged her to go abroad to make *Anastasia* with Ingrid Bergman and Yul Brynner. "You must go," Josh Logan insisted. "You can never find another Charlie. You can never have another Mary. But you can make use of the talent God gave you to make people happy. Get back to acting!"

She finally consented and signed the contract. Things, however, did not go too well. Each morning when she appeared on the set, it was obvious that her mind was elsewhere. "She would learn her lines," said Anatole Litvak, the movie's director. "That wasn't the problem. She didn't seem to know—or care—about their meaning. Once, I told her that she was being an excellent mechanic, that she didn't have the slightest idea of what she was saying.

" 'Please, allow me to try again,' she begged."

Ingrid Bergman was also distressed. "It's practically impossible for Helen Hayes to give a really bad performance," said the Swedish star. "But at first this one seemed to be far below her usual standards. I have always admired her so much. Not only is she a marvelous actress, but she is gracious and compassionate. When the world was up in arms about *Stromboli*, she and Charlie were among the first to send a comforting letter of sympathy and support. Now, it was her time of need. But I didn't know what to do."

Helen realized she was not at her best, and it added to her agony. She was aware that she was giving—the actor's nightmare—a dim performance. "Suddenly," she recalled, "the answer came to me. The faith I needed to carry on meant my returning to the church."

"When she wed Charlie," Marc Connelly said, "the church had disowned her. With him gone and his first wife no longer an obstacle, she confessed her sin in marrying a divorced man. Once again she was about to take communion. She firmly believed that Charlie would understand how badly she needed salvation, that it took the entire Catholic Church to be his understudy."

Following *Anastasia*, Helen accepted an offer to appear on Broadway in the Jean Anouilh romantic comedy *Time Remembered*. Richard Burton was her co-star. She was well aware of his reputation as a womanizer.

One night, Helen, Richard, and nineteen-year-old Susan Strasberg, daughter of the famous drama teachers
Lee and Paula Strasberg, had an after-theatre dinner.
They wound up in Miss Strasberg's hotel suite. Susan,
who had been drinking a great deal of champagne, became violently sick to her stomach. That was when Hel-
en told Burton to leave. "I'll undress poor Susan," she
said. "And put her to bed."

"No," Richard replied. "You go to your room and
leave everything to me!"

"I insist!" Helen said firmly. She had no intention of
leaving the inebriated young girl alone with Burton.
He went.

Comedian Don Rickles visited Helen backstage. She
was surprised when he thanked her for shaping his career. "I was in your daughter's class at the American
Academy of Dramatic Arts," he explained. "I planned
on a dramatic career. But unfortunately I wasn't making
any headway. To help keep my spirits up, I started doing takeoffs on you. Word got back to the director, who
pointed his finger at me and stormed, 'Rickles, I hear
you're making fun of the First Lady of the Theatre! Is
that true?' I tried to deny it, but he was in no mood to be
interrupted.

" 'So all of us can enjoy it,' he continued to bark,
'your class assignment for today is to impersonate her.
Now, get started!'

"As Durante would say, I was mortified, but there
was no way out. I did my Helen Hayes routine. The
director was silent for a minute. Then he applauded.
'Rickles, my boy,' he finally said. 'That's where your
talent lies. Follow your bent, son, you might make it.'
So *Danke schön*, Miss Hayes!"

Helen had her hair dyed snow white for her role in *Time Remembered*. After the show closed, she met Jim in California, where he was finishing a Walt Disney movie. "Jim's hair was even more spectacular than mine," she recalled. It had been cut Indian warrior fashion for his role in *The Light in the Forest*."

"I was chagrined," she admitted, "when he dropped out of Harvard at the end of his sophomore year. But Jim had other ideas. He wanted to be a full-time actor. I'm so very proud that he's developed into a fine and honest one."

Ben Hecht once said about Jim, "Not only does he look like the kid next door, but he makes Jack Armstrong, the All-American boy, seem like a rank imposter."

Young MacArthur has acted successfully in more than a dozen movies and numerous television shows and stage plays. For eleven years, he was highly acclaimed as Detective Danny Williams in the hit series "Hawaii Five-O." A high spot was Helen's appearance on one of the shows. A Chicago reviewer wrote, "What a joy it was to watch those two perform. The grace and skill of the mother—who played Detective Williams' aunt—has visibly rubbed off on the son."

Edward Shaw, a Hollywood producer and close friend, spoke about Jim's complete disinterest in discovering his true identity. "You know he was adopted," Shaw said. "When he turned twenty-one, Helen handed him an envelope containing his adoption papers. 'There's no reason why you shouldn't now learn who your real parents were,' she told him. He took the envelope and tossed it into the fireplace. He said that as he watched it burn, he realized that his real parents had always been Helen and Charles MacArthur."

In the summer of 1958, Helen went to Italy for a private audience with Pope Pius XII. Her son had just become engaged to actress Joyce Bulifant, a pretty blonde he had met in school. His mother took her future daughter-in-law along so that she could rendezvous with Jim in Switzerland, where he was filming a movie. The young couple was married later that year.

Their first child, Charles MacArthur, was born in May 1960. A very happy Helen said, "This is indeed a red-letter day. A bonny grandson with an illustrious name." A few years later Helen became the grandmother of a baby girl, Mary MacArthur. "Both of my grandchildren have been blessed with distinguished names," she said happily.

Jim was divorced in 1967. He next wed actress Melody Patterson, who played the female lead in the television series "F Troop." Helen traveled to Hawaii, where Jim lived, to attend the traditional native ceremony that was performed along the banks of the picturesque Wailu River. This marriage also ended in divorce.

"He'll need a wife like Helen Hayes," Ben Hecht had once predicted. Some one to hold him down. Even though he was adopted, in so many ways he's exactly like Charlie."

Helen enjoys Jim's children tremendously and visits them whenever possible. "Not because they are my grandchildren," she told her lawyer, L. Arnold Weissberger, "but those two really are superior. I predict that when young Charlie reaches middle age, he'll be elected president of the United States—that is, if he wants the job." Then she added, "He'll probably be succeeded by his sister, Mary."

She loves telling stories about them. A favorite occurred several years ago when her grandson watched Helen and Clark Gable in a television showing of *The White Sister*. "The next day," Helen said, "Charlie told his classmate, John Gable, 'I saw your father kissing my grandma last night.' "

When Helen heard about Hecht's death in 1964, she immediately called his widow to offer her condolences. She learned that shortly before Ben died he had expressed a wish to be buried near MacArthur. Nyack cemetery officials turned me down," Ms. Hecht said disconsolately. "They claimed there wasn't any room."

"Let me try," Helen urged the grief-stricken woman.

"She did," said Nunnally Johnson. "After a few minutes of sweet-voiced pontificating, they swiftly managed to find a space—right next to Charlie's grave. Now, those two are together again to engage in some of their hell-raising."

"I'd been told that Helen was fascinated by the lives of America's first ladies," said A.E. Hotchner, author of *The White House*. "We thought she'd be a natural to portray the ten different presidential wives the play called for. I was delighted when she agreed. She made no effort to make herself up to resemble any of them, but you instantly felt that she was ten completely dissimilar women. Outstanding were Abigail Adams, Mary Todd Lincoln, and Edith Wilson."

Morton Gottlieb, the show's producer, said, "I believe the secret of Helen's success is that she's genuinely interested in what makes her characters tick. She's that way with all people. She made me feel that I was an important part of her life. She once gave me a pair of cuff links that had belonged to Charlie. 'He liked them very much,' she said. 'I thought you would like them, too.' "

A few summers later Helen toured the United States and Canada in *The Show Off* and *Right You Are*. Gwyda DonHowe, a member of the cast of both shows, recalled those engagements. "I've acted with lots of stars," she said. "She tops them all. Fans would surround her and ask for autographs. She'd smile and sign their books. Once in Toronto while we were antique hunting, I asked her if she minded all the attention. She quickly replied, 'This is their way of becoming part of the theatre. How could I possibly not cooperate? Besides, I'd worry if they didn't ask.' She's such a contrast to other actresses. Helen only tries to draw the line when it comes to invasion of her personal life."

"Ralph Edwards of *This Is Your Life* wanted to make her the subject of one of his shows," recalled Vincent Price. "He had run one about me and she made an appearance. Now, I wanted to reciprocate. Somehow—I think Jim may have told her—she found out about the projected show. She quickly vetoed it."

She had to be coaxed to participate in a television show celebrating her seventieth birthday. "Who is interested in an old lady like me?" she protested. After some more pressure she agreed to be the narrator on a ninety-minute documentary about her long and spectacular career: *Helen Hayes—Portrait of an American Actress.*

Wisely, she was allowed to describe her own experiences. Jack Gould, the *New York Times* critic, called her appearance, "Vibrant, humorous, perceptive, and nostalgic." A Texas reviewer said, "Last night we were treated to an outstanding performance by an outstanding actress who is also an outstanding American."

Helen, a dedicated member of Actors Equity, joined a picket line outside New York's Lincoln Center. She and other performers were protesting the low salaries paid to dancers from the American Ballet Theatre. As she flashed a V-for-victory sign, she asked Werner Klemperer, once Colonel Klink of "Hogan's Heroes," whether in her declining years she was turning into a radical. Later, she told reporters that she was glad she had come to the aid of the dance group. "Dancers bring so much pleasure to the world," she said simply.

She soon was given the opportunity to appear with one of the most famous of all dancers, Fred Astaire. He and Helen had known each other for many years, but despite careers that went back more than seven decades, they had never worked together. In 1977, when she was seventy-seven and he seventy-eight, NBC decided to star them in Ross Hunter's two-hour television drama "A Family Upside Down." They played the parts of a deeply loving husband and wife forced to live apart because of poor health.

Helen was thrilled to be teamed with Astaire. "You know who would have been happiest?" she asked. "Charlie. He always wanted me to have the chance of acting with Fred, one of his all-time favorites."

The first day on the set, Astaire told his partner, "It's taken us all these years, but we finally made it, kid."

"I guess I'm glad it didn't happen any earlier, laddie," she replied. "Because then I'd have had to be your dancing partner. And with these two left feet that would be too much for you to bear."

Some years back Helen decided to sell Pretty Penny, her twenty-room Nyack home, and dispose of her lifetime treasures. She had them auctioned off for the benefit of the American Academy of Dramatic Arts. "Getting de-thinged," she called it. Out of her hundreds of possessions, she kept for herself only a few mementos. "There's a vanity chair," she said, "that Charlie gave me the first Christmas we knew each other. I'm not parting with that, nor our bed—the four-poster. I'll be needing it to die in."

More than three thousand people attended the two-day sale. They watched more than nine hundred items go on the block: a salad bowl from John Barrymore, a Victorian baby carriage that Maurice Evans had given to Mary when she was born, vases from Katharine Hepburn and Oscar Hammerstein, a glass bird nest that was an anniversary present from John Gielgud, a first edition of *Uncle Tom's Cabin*, paintings and prints by Toulouse-Lautrec, Goya, and Grandma Moses.

Helen attended the first day of the auction. When she noticed a woman handling an antique doll Charlie had bought for Mary on one of their trips to England, she wiped away a tear. Quickly, she dashed over to a tiny wooden chest and pulled out a set of chess pieces that the auctioneers had hidden from souvenir hunters. Muttering at their distrust, she put out the carved pieces on an antique chessboard. When the sale was all over, $57,000 had been raised for the American Academy.

She was pleased when an extremely high bid for the

house fell through. "I guess I really didn't want to sell," she said. "It had been my happy home for so many years. Charlie and the children loved it so. How could I think I'd ever leave it? I must have been dreaming. Pretty Penny has become part of me."

She remained and refurbished the house. She told reporters, "I don't crave work anymore, except for an occasional lark. I acquire new clutter and watch over my roses." One of her "larks" was taking a minor role in a revival of *The Front Page*. "That was a sentimental caper," she explained. "I felt compelled—Charlie was pulling the strings."

In the film *Airport*, Helen played a crusty old lady. For her characterization she received an Oscar as the year's best supporting actress. She had thought that her role in *Airport* would take only two weeks. Instead, she was required to be in Hollywood for five months. At the same time, she taught a seminar in play-reading at the University of Illinois. Once a week she would fly to Chicago to conduct the class.

She joined Jimmy Stewart in recreating *Harvey* for Broadway. She was rehearsing for a benefit performance of Eugene O'Neill's *Long Day's Journey Into Night* when she was hospitalized for an old ailment: her allergy to theatre dust. Cautioned by doctors to quit the stage and take it easy, she reduced her schedule to what Ruth Gordon calls "typical Helen Hayes style—perpetual motion."

As soon as Helen recovered, she appeared in the O'Neill play, collaborated with Anita Loos on a guidebook about New York, played a whimsical old-maid detective in the television series "The Snoop Sisters," starred in the Disney movie *Herbie Rides Again*, and narrated several hour-long television documentaries. While catching her breath, she served as first lector and read from Genesis when Pope John Paul II celebrated a papal mass at Yankee Stadium before eighty thousand communicants.

"That pope's goodness shines from his entire body," she later told Marc Connelly. "The moment you see him it becomes apparent."

"So does yours!" her longtime friend replied.

Epilogue

When Helen Hayes MacArthur neared eighty, she finally agreed to retire and live quietly with her longtime companion-secretary, Vera Bemlian, and her beloved poodles. She now divides her time between her home in Nyack and a small hacienda in Cuernavaca, Mexico. Friends wanted to know what they should do for her birthday. She immediately remarked that they should conduct the festivities at the Actors' Fund Home in Englewood, New Jersey. "I used my birthday celebration for a purpose," she said. "I wanted to publicize the Actors' Fund and to demonstrate how we take care of our own. I joined the fund many years ago. I'm glad there is a retirement home for theatre people. I'll be happy to move in there myself if I ever get to the point when I need help—knock wood."

Helen is not completely inactive. She accepted an invitation from President Jimmy Carter to become a member of the Advisory Committee to the White House Conference on Aging and asked to serve on the council on employment. She said she would like to see that more jobs are found for people beyond the mandatory retirement age who need to work.

A group of retired teachers gave her a standing ovation when she told them employment should be available not only to "well-known, white-haired actresses," but to all old people who can still "do a hand's turn . . . I don't think older people should have extra special privileges. They should have the same standards as anyone else. Jobs should be based on one thing and one thing alone, and that is who can handle the job best. I certainly don't want to discriminate against young people. But I'm just as strongly against reverse discrimination!"

Helen's other big interest is spending time with children. Not long ago she attended a special performance of *The Littlest Clown* at New York's Copacabana ballroom, given by the Pixy Judy Troupe. She was so enthralled with the show about circus clowns, lion tamers, and ballerinas who ride on make-believe horses that she asked if she might join in. As the youngsters, guests of various day-care centers, roared their approval, she pulled a red clown's cap over her white hair. The audience consisted of 275 boys and girls, ranging in age from four to twelve.

Completely attuned to the mood of the young playgoers, Helen made a brief speech. "I'm just going to say that I'm happy to be here because all of you are so beautiful," she told them. She recalled her own, and still vividly remembered first visit to the theatre. "I was five, and I burst out crying when it was over," she confided. "I didn't want it to end." Then she joined her young friends in eating hot dogs and drinking soda pop. She reminisced further about that initial experience. "It was at the National Theatre in Washington, D.C.," she recalled. "The play was *The Merry Widow*. I was in the peanut gallery, way up high. But I could see the wonderful things that were happening on the stage. I wanted to stay there forever. I hope you love the theatre from this moment on and never, never, go away from it in your heart. God bless you."

Later, she told their teachers, "They are such glorious children—but then, all children are. Now, somebody has to follow up and make it possible for them to keep on going to the big shows."

Helen has been a faithful friend and benefactor to another children's project, Father William Wasson's home for orphaned boys and girls located near Mexico City. In addition to raising a great deal of money for the institution, she visits them often. They call her "*Abuelita* Helen," Spanish for "little grandmother Helen."

Speaking of her various activities, she says "What could be more fulfilling than working with the young, the old and keeping alive the memory of Charlie?"

She was thrilled in 1974 when Florida State University established the Charles MacArthur Center for American Theatre. One of its principal goals is the study of writers who have contributed greatly to the theatre but have not been properly recognized. Besides its vast research program, it has set up the Charles MacArthur Award in playwriting to encourage new dramatists.

"The Center hopes to establish itself," said Dean Richard Fallon, "as a force for preserving our dramatic heritage and for bringing a new vitality to the theatre today. An embarrassed Charles MacArthur would probably have greeted our honoring him with a loud Bronx cheer. But I can't think of a better name connected with the American theatre that signifies vitality and inventiveness."

Along with actor Cary Grant, pianist Rudolf Serkin, choreographer Jerome Robbins and musician Count Basie, she recently was awarded a top honor by Washington's Kennedy Center for her "long career of being a beloved performer."

Helen said, "My greatest credit came when I was first called Mrs. Charles MacArthur, [but] I have to admit that I was grateful Charlie and I had our young married life fifty years ago. It was so much easier then. There weren't so many things pulling at young women, at young couples. In fact, there used to be a cliché that before you got married everyone conspired to keep you apart—which was never more true than in my and Charlie's case. But after you were married, the whole world conspired to keep you together. I think it is so much harder now, especially for a young woman who wants a great deal from life. I don't know how I'd manage if I were a young woman starting a career and family today."

Then the First Lady of the Theatre thought a moment and added, "I guess I would do just as I did before. I would decide on what really mattered to me and fight for it all the way."

Helen spends the winter months in Mexico. "In Cuernavaca I can see two snow-capped volcanoes from my veranda," she said. Only in Mexico we call it a *galeria*. They seem to be saying, 'Be humble in God's presence,' and that is my prayer. I have breakfast outdoors, looking at the volcanoes."

Then José, her gardener, brings the morning newspaper. Next comes a stroll into the village, where she does some marketing. Perhaps a stop to visit old friends who are living where it is pleasant and cheap. She plays bridge, does a few laps in her swimming pool. She is invited to a great many parties but goes only to the ones given by intimates—"people I love."

Not long ago she had two accidents. The first time, she was running through the dark to rescue one of her poodles that had slipped into the swimming pool. She stumbled over an ancient Aztec statue and bruised a knee. Then she fell again, skidding on the wet slippery flagstones of a marketplace. She had a bumped nose, bruised elbows, and a torn ligament in her right leg.

"Charlie would have helped me up," she said, "brushed me off, and whispered sweetly, 'Better stay off the sauce, Helen.' Just before we married, he held my hand and sighed, 'Maybe with me you will never be rich, but I promise that you will never be bored.'

"Again, he was so right. I never was. I never shall be. He is with me always."

Acknowledgments

Many people generously shared their Hayes-MacArthur memories with me. In Nyack, N.Y.; Hollywood; Washington, D.C.; New York City; Scranton, Pa.; and Chicago, I talked to friends, relatives, associates, and neighbors of this remarkable couple. The interviews were conducted while I was working on the book or earlier when I wrote newspaper and magazine stories about Helen Hayes MacArthur. The list is long. Undoubtedly, I have omitted some names. To those people my sincerest apologies and profound thanks.

I am also indebted to Vincent Price, Ingrid Bergman, Roderick MacArthur, Dean Richard Fallon, Maurice Zolotow, Barbara Boll Herndon, Fred Astaire, Richard Burton, Edward Shaw, Phyllis Cerf Wagner, Margaret Boll, Gwyda DonHowe, Elaine Whitelaw, Mike Rotunno, Abe Stern, A. E. Hotchner, Morton Gottlieb, Larry Monnarino, Lillian Gish, José Ferrer, Averell Harriman, Father George Reinheimer, Roger Kostmayer,

Mary Martin, Murray Abraham, Colleen Dewhurst, Edgar Leighton, Molly Picon, Clifton Hamilton, William Cavanaugh, Andrew Neuman, John Lindsay, Dr. Jonas Salk, Alice Cahill, Josh Logan, Constance Bessie, Victor Boesen, Maureen Stapleton, Ethel Merman, Ike Haigler, Sadie Geller, Lorenzo Del Vechio, Harry Prugh and Carl Gartner.

Many others were extremely helpful. I am grateful to June Reno for her editing skill and valuable suggestions; Louise Samuels of Cuernavaca, Mexico, who furnished me with much worthwhile material from that region; her husband, Charlie Samuels, a protégé of Ben Hecht, who lived near me in Nyack and regaled me with hilarious Hecht and MacArthur tales; Greg Jacobsen and Roberta Corbett for supplying useful research from Hollywood and Chicago; librarians of the Academy of Motion Picture Arts and Sciences, the Lincoln Center for the Performing Arts, the Charles MacArthur Center for Development of American Theatre, the Nyack Library, the American Film Institute, the UCLA Theatre Library, the University of Wisconsin Center for Film and Theatre Research, the *Rockland Journal News*, and the *Chicago Tribune*; and Anne Angelo for typing the final manuscript.

I was very fortunate in being able to spend some time with Marc Connelly shortly before his death. The distinguished playwright was approaching his ninetieth birthday. He had won a Pultizer Prize in 1930 for what has become a classic of the American stage, *The Green Pastures*. He told me, "It's practically impossible to think of Charlie's life in chronological order. He didn't live that way." Midway through this book I discovered that Connelly was quite right. In addition to providing me with delightful, if slightly disarranged, anecdotes, he pointed me to many excellent sources. Following these acknowledgments the reader will find a bibliographical list of the books I consulted. I offer my deepfelt appreciation to the authors.

The final words are reserved for my wife, Sallie Prugh Robbins. I am beholden to her for good advice, encouragement, enthusiasm, and enduring my endless conversations about Helen Hayes and Charles MacArthur.

Bibliography

Adams, Samuel Hopkins. *A. Woollcott*. New York: Reynall and Hitchcock, 1945.

Bankhead, Tallulah. *My Autobiography*. New York: Harper's, 1952.

Barnes, Eric Woolencott. *The Man Who Lived Twice—Edward Sheldon*. New York: Scribners, 1956.

Barris, Alex. *Stop the Presses*. New York: Barnes, 1976.

Behrman, S. N. *People in a Diary*. Boston: Little, Brown, 1972.

Benchley, Nathaniel. *Robert Benchley*, New York: McGraw-Hill, 1955.

Brown, Catherine Hayes. *Letters to Mary*. Foreword by Charles MacArthur. New York: Random House, 1940.

Brown, John Mason. *Mirror to His Times: The Worlds of Robert E. Sherwood*. New York: Harper and Row, 1956.

Butcher, Fanny. *Many Lives—One Love*. New York: Harper and Row, 1972.

Carter, Richard. *Breakthrough: The Saga of Jonas Salk*. New York: Trident Press, 1966.

Cerf, Bennett. *Bumper Crop*. New York: Garden City Books, 1956.

Connelly, Marcus Cook. *Voices Offstage*. New York: Holt, Rinehart and Winston, 1968.

Corliss, Richard. *Talking Pictures: Screenwriters in the American Cinema*. Woodstock, N.Y.: Overlook Press, 1968.

Dorlag, Arthur, and Irvine, John, eds. *The Stage Works of Charles MacArthur*. Tallahassee: Florida State University Foundation, 1974.

Drennen, Robert, ed. *The Algonquin Wits*. New York: Citadel Press, 1968.

Edmiston, Susan, and Cirino, Linda. *Literary New York*. Boston: Houghton Mifflin, 1976.

Eels, George. *Hedda and Louella*. New York: Putnam's, 1972.

Fowler, Gene. *Good Night Sweet Prince: The Life and Times of John Barrymore*. New York: Viking, 1944.

_____. *Skyline*. New York: Viking, 1961.

Gassner, John, and Nichols, Dudley, eds. *Twenty Best Film Plays*. New York: Crown, 1943.

Gish, Lillian, with Pinchot, Ann. *Lillian Gish: The Movies, Mr. Griffith, and Me*. Englewood Cliffs, N.J., Prentice-Hall, 1969.

Gordon, Ruth. *Myself Among Others*. New York: Atheneum, 1971.

_____. *My Side*. New York: Harper and Row, 1976.

_____. *An Open Book*. New York: Doubleday, 1980.

Guiles, Fred Lawrence. *Hanging On in Paradise*. New York: McGraw-Hill, 1975.

Hansen, Harry. *Midwest Portraits*. New York: Harcourt, Brace, 1923.

Harriman, Margaret Case. *The Vicious Circle: The Story of the Algonquin Round Table*. New York: Rinehart, 1951.

_____. *Blessed Are the Debonair*. New York: Rinehart, 1956.

Harris, Jed. *A Dance On the High Wire*. New York: Crown, 1979.

Hayes, Helen, and Kennedy, Mary. *Star on Her Forehead*. New York: Dodd Mead, 1949.

_____, with Funke, Lewis. *A Gift of Joy*. New York: Evans, 1965.

_____, with Doty, Sanford. *On Reflection*. New York: Evans, 1968.

_____, and Loos, Anita. *Twice Over Lightly*. New York: Harcourt Brace Jovanovich, 1972.

Hecht, Ben. *Charlie*. New York: Harper and Brothers, 1957.

Hoffman, William. *The Stockholder—John MacArthur*. New York: Lyle Stuart, 1969.

Hoyt, Edwin. *Alexander Woollcott*. New York: Abelard-Schuman, 1968.

Hughes, Glenn. *A History of the American Theatre—1700 to 1950*. New York: Samuel French, 1951.

Johnson, Doris. *The Letters of Nunally Johnson*. New York: Knopf, 1981.

Johnson, Nora. *Flashback—Nunnally Johnson*. New York: Doubleday, 1979.

Kahn, E. J., Jr. *The World of Swope*. New York: Simon and Schuster, 1965.

Kaufman, Beatrice, and Hennessy, Joseph, eds. *The*

Letters of Alexander Woollcott. New York: Viking, 1944.

Kaytor, Marilyn. *21: The Life and Times of New York's Favorite Club*. New York: Viking, 1975.

Keats, John. *You Might as Well Live: The Life and Times of Dorothy Parker*. New York: Simon and Schuster, 1970.

Kobler, John. *Damned in Paradise: The Life of John Barrymore*. New York: Atheneum, 1977.

Krutch, Joseph Wood. *American Drama Since 1918*. New York: Random House, 1939.

Lasky, Jesse, with Weldon, Don. *I Blow My Own Horn*. New York: Doubleday, 1957.

Logan, Joshua. *Josh*. New York: Delacorte, 1976.

MacArthur, Charles. *War Bugs*. New York: Doubleday, Doran, 1929.

McPhaul, John. *Deadlines and Monkeyshines: The Fabled World of Chicago Journalism*. Englewood Cliffs, N.J.: Prentice-Hall, 1962.

Maney, Richard. *Fanfare: The Confessions of a Press Agent*. New York: Harper and Brothers, 1957.

Marx, Arthur. *Life with Groucho*. New York: Simon and Schuster, 1954.

_____. *Goldwyn*. New York: Norton, 1976.

Marx, Harpo, and Barber, Rowland. *Harpo Speaks*. New York: Bernard Geis, 1961.

Meredith, Scott. *George S. Kaufman and His Friends*. New York: Doublday, 1974.

Nathan, George Jean. *Encyclopedia of the Theatre*. New York: Knopf, 1940.

Newquist, Roy. *Showcase*. New York: William Morrow, 1946.

Nolan, Paul. *Marc Connelly*. New York: Twayne, 1969.

O'Connor, Richard. *Heyward Broun.* New York: Putnam's, 1975.

Rosmond, Babette. *Robert Benchley: His Life and Good Times.* New York: Doubleday, 1970.

Sardi, Vincent, and Gehman, Richard. *Sardi's.* New York: Henry Holt, 1953.

Smith, H. Allen. *The Life and Legend of Gene Fowler.* New York: William Morrow, 1972.

Sobel, Louis. *The Longest Street.* New York: Crown, 1968.

Strasberg, Susan. *Bitter Sweet.* New York: Putnam's, 1980.

Teichmann, Howard. *George S. Kaufman, An Intimate Portrait.* New York: Atheneum, 1972.

_____. *Smart Aleck: The Wit, World and Life of Alexander Woollcott.* New York: William Morrow, 1976.

Thomas, Bob. *Joan Crawford.* New York: Simon and Schuster, 1978.

Woollcott, Alexander. *Long, Long Ago.* New York: Viking, 1943.

Yates, Norris. *Robert Benchley.* New York: Twayne, 1968.

Zolotow, Maruice. *Stagestruck: The Romance of Alfred Lunt and Lynn Fontanne.* New York: Harcourt, Brace and World, 1964.

Index